In Public Restrooms \ 2007-2014

Birk Weiberg \ 2015

Bibliographic information published by the Deutsche Nationalbibliothek
The Deutsche Nationalbibliothek lists this publication in the Deutsche Nationalbibliografie;
detailed bibliographic data are available on the Internet at http://dnb.dnb.de.

© 2015 Birk Weiberg

BoD – Books on Demand, Norderstedt
ISBN 9783738643374

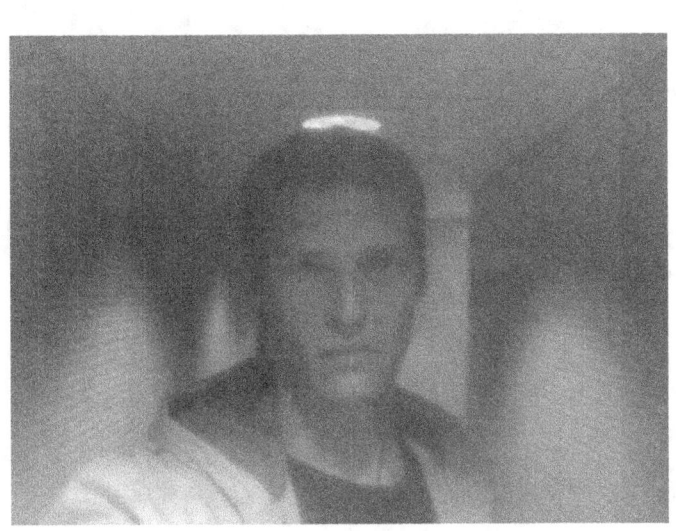

```
ExifTool Version Number         : 10.05
File Name                       : 070408_150307.jpg
Directory                       : ../Selection
File Size                       : 105 kB
File Modification Date/Time     : 2007:04:09 09:28:29+02:00
File Access Date/Time           : 2015:11:29 14:04:25+01:00
File Inode Change Date/Time     : 2015:11:05 21:35:08+01:00
File Permissions                : rw-r--r--
File Type                       : JPEG
File Type Extension             : jpg
MIME Type                       : image/jpeg
JFIF Version                    : 1.02
Resolution Unit                 : None
X Resolution                    : 1
Y Resolution                    : 1
Image Width                     : 1280
Image Height                    : 960
Encoding Process                : Baseline DCT, Huffman coding
Bits Per Sample                 : 8
Color Components                : 3
Y Cb Cr Sub Sampling            : YCbCr4:2:2 (2 1)
Image Size                      : 1280x960
Megapixels                      : 1.2
```

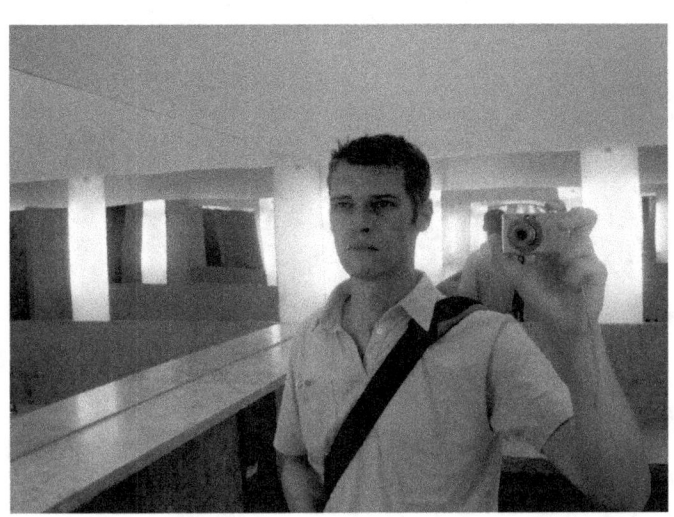

```
ExifTool Version Number         : 10.05
File Name                       : IMG_5960.JPG
Directory                       : ../Selection
File Size                       : 564 kB
File Modification Date/Time     : 2007:06:08 17:27:54+02:00
File Access Date/Time           : 2015:11:29 14:04:25+01:00
File Inode Change Date/Time     : 2015:11:05 21:35:08+01:00
File Permissions                : rw-r--r--
File Type                       : JPEG
File Type Extension             : jpg
MIME Type                       : image/jpeg
Exif Byte Order                 : Little-endian (Intel, II)
Make                            : Canon
Camera Model Name               : Canon DIGITAL IXUS 50
Orientation                     : Horizontal (normal)
X Resolution                    : 180
Y Resolution                    : 180
Resolution Unit                 : inches
Modify Date                     : 2007:06:06 13:24:54
Y Cb Cr Positioning             : Centered
Exposure Time                   : 1/80
F Number                        : 2.8
Exif Version                    : 0220
Date/Time Original              : 2007:06:06 13:24:54
Create Date                     : 2007:06:06 13:24:54
Components Configuration        : Y, Cb, Cr, -
Compressed Bits Per Pixel       : 3
Shutter Speed Value             : 1/79
Aperture Value                  : 2.8
Max Aperture Value              : 2.8
Flash                           : Off, Did not fire
Focal Length                    : 5.8 mm
Macro Mode                      : Normal
Self Timer                      : Off
Quality                         : Fine
Canon Flash Mode                : Off
Continuous Drive                : Single
Focus Mode                      : Single
Record Mode                     : JPEG
Canon Image Size                : Medium 1
Easy Mode                       : Full auto
Digital Zoom                    : None
Contrast                        : Normal
Saturation                      : Normal
Sharpness                       : 0
Camera ISO                      : Auto
Metering Mode                   : Evaluative
Focus Range                     : Auto
AF Point                        : Auto AF point selection
Canon Exposure Mode             : Easy
Lens Type                       : n/a
Max Focal Length                : 17.4 mm
Min Focal Length                : 5.8 mm
Focal Units                     : 1000/mm
Max Aperture                    : 2.8
Min Aperture                    : 5.6
Flash Bits                      : (none)
Focus Continuous                : Single
AE Setting                      : Normal AE
Zoom Source Width               : 2592
Zoom Target Width               : 2592
Spot Metering Mode              : Center
Photo Effect                    : Off
Manual Flash Output             : n/a
Focal Type                      : Zoom
Focal Plane X Size              : 5.84 mm
Focal Plane Y Size              : 4.37 mm
Auto ISO                        : 100
Base ISO                        : 50
Measured EV                     : 10.41
Target Aperture                 : 2.8
Target Exposure Time            : 1/79
Exposure Compensation           : 0
White Balance                   : Auto
Slow Shutter                    : Off
Shot Number In Continuous Burst : 0
Optical Zoom Code               : 0
Flash Guide Number              : 0
Flash Exposure Compensation     : 0
Auto Exposure Bracketing        : Off
AEB Bracket Value               : 0
Control Mode                    : Camera Local Control
Focus Distance Upper            : 1.57 m
Focus Distance Lower            : 0 m
Bulb Duration                   : 0
Camera Type                     : Compact
```

```
Auto Rotate                          : None
ND Filter                            : Off
Self Timer 2                         : 0
Flash Output                         : 0
Num AF Points                        : 9
Valid AF Points                      : 9
Canon Image Width                    : 2048
Canon Image Height                   : 1536
AF Image Width                       : 1296
AF Image Height                      : 242
AF Area Width                        : 233
AF Area Height                       : 44
AF Area X Positions                  : -233 0 233 -233 0 233 -233 0 233
AF Area Y Positions                  : -45 -45 -45 0 0 0 45 45 45
AF Points In Focus                   : 4
Primary AF Point                     : 4
Thumbnail Image Valid Area           : 0 0 0 0
Canon Image Type                     : IMG:DIGITAL IXUS 50 JPEG
Canon Firmware Version               : Firmware Version 1.01
File Number                          : 159-5960
Owner Name                           :
Canon Model ID                       : PowerShot SD400 / Digital IXUS 50 / IXY Digital 55
Camera Temperature                   : 36 C
Date Stamp Mode                      : Off
My Color Mode                        : Off
Firmware Revision                    : 1.01 rev 2.00
User Comment                         :
Flashpix Version                     : 0100
Color Space                          : sRGB
Exif Image Width                     : 2048
Exif Image Height                    : 1536
Interoperability Index               : R98 - DCF basic file (sRGB)
Interoperability Version             : 0100
Related Image Width                  : 2048
Related Image Height                 : 1536
Focal Plane X Resolution             : 9102.222222
Focal Plane Y Resolution             : 9142.857143
Focal Plane Resolution Unit          : inches
Sensing Method                       : One-chip color area
File Source                          : Digital Camera
Custom Rendered                      : Normal
Exposure Mode                        : Auto
Digital Zoom Ratio                   : 1
Scene Capture Type                   : Standard
Compression                          : JPEG (old-style)
Thumbnail Offset                     : 5120
Thumbnail Length                     : 3958
Profile CMM Type                     : appl
Profile Version                      : 2.2.0
Profile Class                        : Input Device Profile
Color Space Data                     : RGB
Profile Connection Space             : XYZ
Profile Date Time                    : 2003:07:01 00:00:00
Profile File Signature               : acsp
Primary Platform                     : Apple Computer Inc.
CMM Flags                            : Not Embedded, Independent
Device Manufacturer                  : appl
Device Model                         :
Device Attributes                    : Reflective, Glossy, Positive, Color
Rendering Intent                     : Perceptual
Connection Space Illuminant          : 0.9642 1 0.82491
Profile Creator                      : appl
Profile ID                           : 0
Red Matrix Column                    : 0.45427 0.24263 0.01482
Green Matrix Column                  : 0.35332 0.67441 0.09042
Blue Matrix Column                   : 0.15662 0.08336 0.71953
Media White Point                    : 0.95047 1 1.0891
Chromatic Adaptation                 : 1.04788 0.02292 -0.0502 0.02957 0.99049 -0.01706 -0.00923 0.01508 0.75165
Red Tone Reproduction Curve          : (Binary data 14 bytes, use -b option to extract)
Green Tone Reproduction Curve        : (Binary data 14 bytes, use -b option to extract)
Blue Tone Reproduction Curve         : (Binary data 14 bytes, use -b option to extract)
Profile Description                  : Camera RGB Profile
Profile Copyright                    : Copyright 2003 Apple Computer Inc., all rights reserved.
Profile Description ML               : Camera RGB Profile
Profile Description ML (es-ES)       : Perfil RGB para Cámara
Profile Description ML (da-DK)       : RGB-beskrivelse til Kamera
Profile Description ML (de-DE)       : RGB-Profil für Kameras
Profile Description ML (fi-FI)       : Kameran RGB-profiili
Profile Description ML (fr-FU)       : Profil RVB de l'appareil-photo
Profile Description ML (it-IT)       : Profilo RGB Fotocamera
Profile Description ML (nl-NL)       : RGB-profiel Camera
Profile Description ML (no-NO)       : RGB-kameraprofil
Profile Description ML (pt-BR)       : Perfil RGB de Câmera
Profile Description ML (sv-SE)       : RGB-profil för Kamera
Profile Description ML (ja-JP)       : カメラ RGB プロファイル
Profile Description ML (ko-KR)       : 카메라 RGB 프로파일
```

```
Profile Description ML (zh-TW)   : 數位相機 RGB 色彩描述
Profile Description ML (zh-CN)   : 相机 RGB 描述文件
Image Width                      : 2048
Image Height                     : 1536
Encoding Process                 : Baseline DCT, Huffman coding
Bits Per Sample                  : 8
Color Components                 : 3
Y Cb Cr Sub Sampling             : YCbCr4:2:2 (2 1)
Aperture                         : 2.8
Drive Mode                       : Single-frame Shooting
ISO                              : 50
Image Size                       : 2048x1536
Lens                             : 5.8 - 17.4 mm
Lens ID                          : Unknown 5-17mm
Megapixels                       : 3.1
Scale Factor To 35 mm Equivalent : 6.1
Shooting Mode                    : Full auto
Shutter Speed                    : 1/80
Thumbnail Image                  : (Binary data 3958 bytes, use -b option to extract)
Circle Of Confusion              : 0.005 mm
Depth Of Field                   : 0.56 m (0.59 - 1.16 m)
Field Of View                    : 54.2 deg
Focal Length                     : 5.8 mm (35 mm equivalent: 35.2 mm)
Hyperfocal Distance              : 2.43 m
Lens                             : 5.8 - 17.4 mm (35 mm equivalent: 35.2 - 105.6 mm)
Light Value                      : 10.3
```

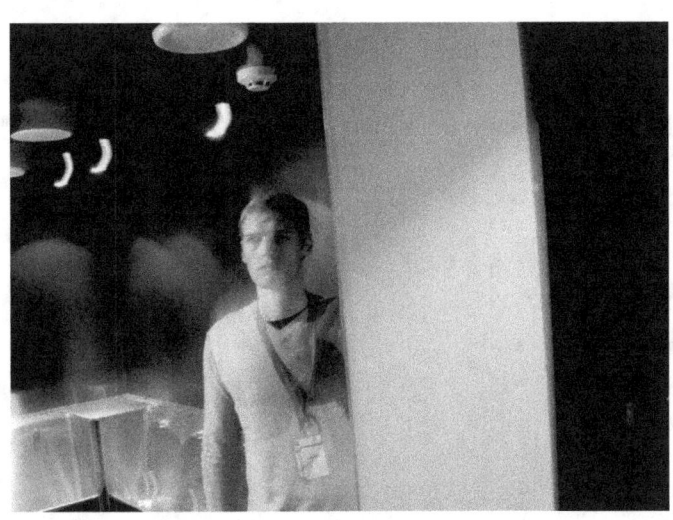

```
ExifTool Version Number         : 10.05
File Name                       : DSC00642.JPG
Directory                       : ../Selection
File Size                       : 1803 kB
File Modification Date/Time     : 2007:11:08 23:50:56+01:00
File Access Date/Time           : 2015:11:29 14:04:25+01:00
File Inode Change Date/Time     : 2015:11:05 21:35:08+01:00
File Permissions                : rw-r--r--
File Type                       : JPEG
File Type Extension             : jpg
MIME Type                       : image/jpeg
Exif Byte Order                 : Little-endian (Intel, II)
Image Description               :
Make                            : SONY
Camera Model Name               : DSC-W80
Orientation                     : Horizontal (normal)
X Resolution                    : 72
Y Resolution                    : 72
Resolution Unit                 : inches
Modify Date                     : 2007:11:07 02:24:11
Y Cb Cr Positioning             : Co-sited
Exposure Time                   : 0.3
F Number                        : 2.8
Exposure Program                : Program AE
ISO                             : 400
Exif Version                    : 0221
Date/Time Original              : 2007:11:07 02:24:11
Create Date                     : 2007:11:07 02:24:11
Components Configuration        : Y, Cb, Cr, -
Compressed Bits Per Pixel       : 4
Exposure Compensation           : 0
Max Aperture Value              : 2.8
Metering Mode                   : Multi-segment
Light Source                    : Unknown
Flash                           : Off, Did not fire
Focal Length                    : 5.8 mm
Creative Style                  : Standard
Macro                           : On
Focus Mode                      : AF-S
AF Area Mode                    : Multi
AF Illuminator                  : Auto
JPEG Quality                    : Standard
Flash Level                     : Normal
Release Mode                    : Normal
Sequence Number                 : Single
Anti-Blur                       : On (Continuous)
Flashpix Version                : 0100
Color Space                     : sRGB
Exif Image Width                : 2592
Exif Image Height               : 1944
Interoperability Index          : R98 - DCF basic file (sRGB)
Interoperability Version        : 0100
File Source                     : Digital Camera
Scene Type                      : Directly photographed
Custom Rendered                 : Normal
Exposure Mode                   : Auto
White Balance                   : Auto
Scene Capture Type              : Standard
Contrast                        : Normal
Saturation                      : Normal
Sharpness                       : Normal
PrintIM Version                 : 0300
Compression                     : JPEG (old-style)
Thumbnail Offset                : 9384
Thumbnail Length                : 8166
Profile CMM Type                : appl
Profile Version                 : 2.2.0
Profile Class                   : Input Device Profile
Color Space Data                : RGB
Profile Connection Space        : XYZ
Profile Date Time               : 2003:07:01 00:00:00
Profile File Signature          : acsp
Primary Platform                : Apple Computer Inc.
CMM Flags                       : Not Embedded, Independent
Device Manufacturer             : appl
Device Model                    :
Device Attributes               : Reflective, Glossy, Positive, Color
Rendering Intent                : Perceptual
Connection Space Illuminant     : 0.9642 1 0.82491
Profile Creator                 : appl
Profile ID                      : 0
Red Matrix Column               : 0.45427 0.24263 0.01482
Green Matrix Column             : 0.35332 0.67441 0.09042
Blue Matrix Column              : 0.15662 0.08336 0.71953
Media White Point               : 0.95047 1 1.0891
Chromatic Adaptation            : 1.04788 0.02292 -0.0502 0.02957 0.99049 -0.01706 -0.00923 0.01508 0.75165
```

```
Red Tone Reproduction Curve      : (Binary data 14 bytes, use -b option to extract)
Green Tone Reproduction Curve    : (Binary data 14 bytes, use -b option to extract)
Blue Tone Reproduction Curve     : (Binary data 14 bytes, use -b option to extract)
Profile Description              : Camera RGB Profile
Profile Copyright                : Copyright 2003 Apple Computer Inc., all rights reserved.
Profile Description ML           : Camera RGB Profile
Profile Description ML (es-ES)   : Perfil RGB para Cámara
Profile Description ML (da-DK)   : RGB-beskrivelse til Kamera
Profile Description ML (de-DE)   : RGB-Profil für Kameras
Profile Description ML (fi-FI)   : Kameran RGB-profiili
Profile Description ML (fr-FU)   : Profil RVB de l'appareil-photo
Profile Description ML (it-IT)   : Profilo RGB Fotocamera
Profile Description ML (nl-NL)   : RGB-profiel Camera
Profile Description ML (no-NO)   : RGB-kameraprofil
Profile Description ML (pt-BR)   : Perfil RGB de Câmera
Profile Description ML (sv-SE)   : RGB-profil för Kamera
Profile Description ML (ja-JP)   : カメラ RGB プロファイル
Profile Description ML (ko-KR)   : 카메라 RGB 프로파일
Profile Description ML (zh-TW)   : 數位相機 RGB 色彩描述
Profile Description ML (zh-CN)   : 相机 RGB 描述文件
Image Width                      : 2592
Image Height                     : 1944
Encoding Process                 : Baseline DCT, Huffman coding
Bits Per Sample                  : 8
Color Components                 : 3
Y Cb Cr Sub Sampling             : YCbCr4:2:2 (2 1)
Aperture                         : 2.8
Image Size                       : 2592x1944
Megapixels                       : 5.0
Shutter Speed                    : 0.3
Thumbnail Image                  : (Binary data 8166 bytes, use -b option to extract)
Focal Length                     : 5.8 mm
Light Value                      : 2.6
```

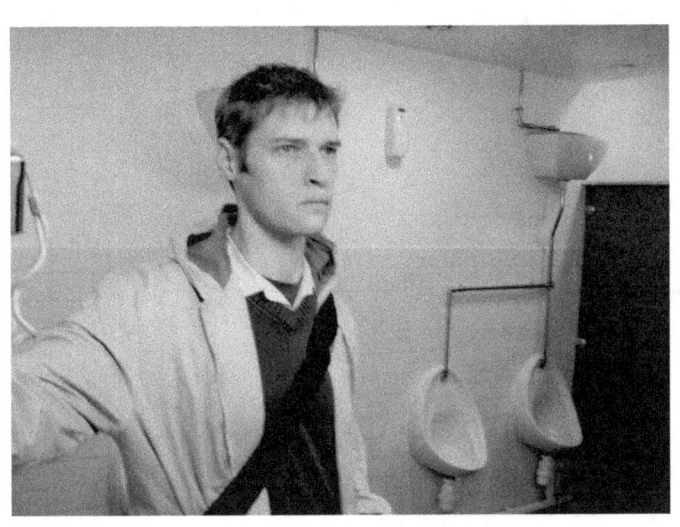

```
ExifTool Version Number         : 10.05
File Name                       : DSC00707.JPG
Directory                       : ../Selection
File Size                       : 1711 kB
File Modification Date/Time     : 2007:11:08 23:51:18+01:00
File Access Date/Time           : 2015:11:29 14:04:26+01:00
File Inode Change Date/Time     : 2015:11:05 21:35:08+01:00
File Permissions                : rw-r--r--
File Type                       : JPEG
File Type Extension             : jpg
MIME Type                       : image/jpeg
Exif Byte Order                 : Little-endian (Intel, II)
Image Description               :
Make                            : SONY
Camera Model Name               : DSC-W80
Orientation                     : Horizontal (normal)
X Resolution                    : 72
Y Resolution                    : 72
Resolution Unit                 : inches
Modify Date                     : 2007:11:08 12:59:39
Y Cb Cr Positioning             : Co-sited
Exposure Time                   : 1/30
F Number                        : 2.8
Exposure Program                : Program AE
ISO                             : 400
Exif Version                    : 0221
Date/Time Original              : 2007:11:08 12:59:39
Create Date                     : 2007:11:08 12:59:39
Components Configuration        : Y, Cb, Cr, -
Compressed Bits Per Pixel       : 4
Exposure Compensation           : 0
Max Aperture Value              : 2.8
Metering Mode                   : Multi-segment
Light Source                    : Unknown
Flash                           : Off, Did not fire
Focal Length                    : 5.8 mm
Creative Style                  : Standard
Macro                           : Off
Focus Mode                      : AF-S
AF Area Mode                    : Multi
AF Illuminator                  : Auto
JPEG Quality                    : Standard
Flash Level                     : Normal
Release Mode                    : Normal
Sequence Number                 : Single
Anti-Blur                       : On (Continuous)
Flashpix Version                : 0100
Color Space                     : sRGB
Exif Image Width                : 2592
Exif Image Height               : 1944
Interoperability Index          : R98 - DCF basic file (sRGB)
Interoperability Version        : 0100
File Source                     : Digital Camera
Scene Type                      : Directly photographed
Custom Rendered                 : Normal
Exposure Mode                   : Auto
White Balance                   : Auto
Scene Capture Type              : Standard
Contrast                        : Normal
Saturation                      : Normal
Sharpness                       : Normal
PrintIM Version                 : 0300
Compression                     : JPEG (old-style)
Thumbnail Offset                : 9384
Thumbnail Length                : 9037
Profile CMM Type                : appl
Profile Version                 : 2.2.0
Profile Class                   : Input Device Profile
Color Space Data                : RGB
Profile Connection Space        : XYZ
Profile Date Time               : 2003:07:01 00:00:00
Profile File Signature          : acsp
Primary Platform                : Apple Computer Inc.
CMM Flags                       : Not Embedded, Independent
Device Manufacturer             : appl
Device Model                    :
Device Attributes               : Reflective, Glossy, Positive, Color
Rendering Intent                : Perceptual
Connection Space Illuminant     : 0.9642 1 0.82491
Profile Creator                 : appl
Profile ID                      : 0
Red Matrix Column               : 0.45427 0.24263 0.01482
Green Matrix Column             : 0.35332 0.67441 0.09042
Blue Matrix Column              : 0.15662 0.08336 0.71953
Media White Point               : 0.95047 1 1.0891
Chromatic Adaptation            : 1.04788 0.02292 -0.0502 0.02957 0.99049 -0.01706 -0.00923 0.01508 0.75165
```

```
Red Tone Reproduction Curve      : (Binary data 14 bytes, use -b option to extract)
Green Tone Reproduction Curve    : (Binary data 14 bytes, use -b option to extract)
Blue Tone Reproduction Curve     : (Binary data 14 bytes, use -b option to extract)
Profile Description              : Camera RGB Profile
Profile Copyright                : Copyright 2003 Apple Computer Inc., all rights reserved.
Profile Description ML           : Camera RGB Profile
Profile Description ML (es-ES)   : Perfil RGB para Cámara
Profile Description ML (da-DK)   : RGB-beskrivelse til Kamera
Profile Description ML (de-DE)   : RGB-Profil für Kameras
Profile Description ML (fi-FI)   : Kameran RGB-profiili
Profile Description ML (fr-FU)   : Profil RVB de l'appareil-photo
Profile Description ML (it-IT)   : Profilo RGB Fotocamera
Profile Description ML (nl-NL)   : RGB-profiel Camera
Profile Description ML (no-NO)   : RGB-kameraprofil
Profile Description ML (pt-BR)   : Perfil RGB de Câmera
Profile Description ML (sv-SE)   : RGB-profil för Kamera
Profile Description ML (ja-JP)   : カメラ RGB プロファイル
Profile Description ML (ko-KR)   : 카메라 RGB 프로파일
Profile Description ML (zh-TW)   : 數位相機 RGB 色彩描述
Profile Description ML (zh-CN)   : 相机 RGB 描述文件
Image Width                      : 2592
Image Height                     : 1944
Encoding Process                 : Baseline DCT, Huffman coding
Bits Per Sample                  : 8
Color Components                 : 3
Y Cb Cr Sub Sampling             : YCbCr4:2:2 (2 1)
Aperture                         : 2.8
Image Size                       : 2592x1944
Megapixels                       : 5.0
Shutter Speed                    : 1/30
Thumbnail Image                  : (Binary data 9037 bytes, use -b option to extract)
Focal Length                     : 5.8 mm
Light Value                      : 5.9
```

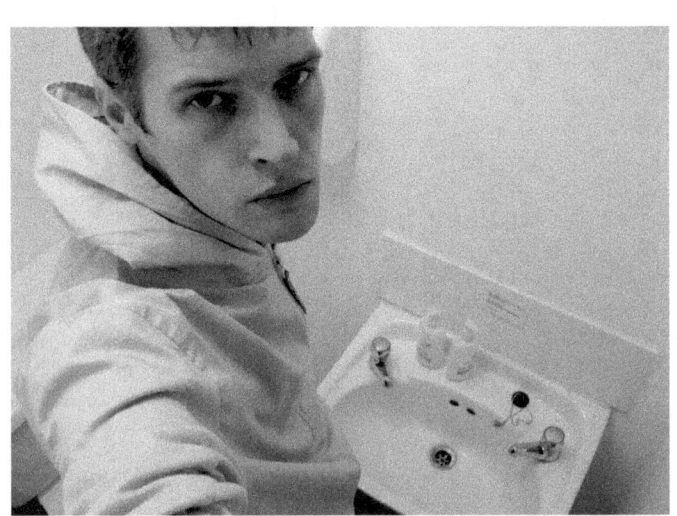

```
ExifTool Version Number        : 10.05
File Name                      : DSC00732.JPG
Directory                      : ../Selection
File Size                      : 1498 kB
File Modification Date/Time    : 2007:11:17 09:05:23+01:00
File Access Date/Time          : 2015:11:29 14:04:26+01:00
File Inode Change Date/Time    : 2015:11:05 21:35:08+01:00
File Permissions               : rw-r--r--
File Type                      : JPEG
File Type Extension            : jpg
MIME Type                      : image/jpeg
Exif Byte Order                : Big-endian (Motorola, MM)
Make                           : SONY
Camera Model Name              : DSC-W80
Orientation                    : Horizontal (normal)
X Resolution                   : 72
Y Resolution                   : 72
Resolution Unit                : inches
Software                       : QuickTime 7.3
Modify Date                    : 2007:11:17 09:05:22
Host Computer                  : Mac OS X 10.5.1
Y Cb Cr Positioning            : Centered
Exposure Time                  : 1/50
F Number                       : 2.8
Exposure Program               : Program AE
ISO                            : 125
Exif Version                   : 0220
Date/Time Original             : 2007:11:08 16:48:30
Create Date                    : 2007:11:08 16:48:30
Exposure Compensation          : 0
Max Aperture Value             : 2.8
Metering Mode                  : Multi-segment
Light Source                   : Unknown
Flash                          : Off, Did not fire
Focal Length                   : 5.8 mm
Color Space                    : sRGB
Compression                    : JPEG (old-style)
Thumbnail Offset               : 610
Thumbnail Length               : 3854
Comment                        : AppleMark.
Image Width                    : 2592
Image Height                   : 1944
Encoding Process               : Baseline DCT, Huffman coding
Bits Per Sample                : 8
Color Components               : 3
Y Cb Cr Sub Sampling           : YCbCr4:2:2 (2 1)
Profile CMM Type               : appl
Profile Version                : 2.2.0
Profile Class                  : Input Device Profile
Color Space Data               : RGB
Profile Connection Space       : XYZ
Profile Date Time              : 2003:07:01 00:00:00
Profile File Signature         : acsp
Primary Platform               : Apple Computer Inc.
CMM Flags                      : Not Embedded, Independent
Device Manufacturer            : appl
Device Model                   :
Device Attributes              : Reflective, Glossy, Positive, Color
Rendering Intent               : Perceptual
Connection Space Illuminant    : 0.9642 1 0.82491
Profile Creator                : appl
Profile ID                     : 0
Red Matrix Column              : 0.45427 0.24263 0.01482
Green Matrix Column            : 0.35332 0.67441 0.09042
Blue Matrix Column             : 0.15662 0.08336 0.71953
Media White Point              : 0.95047 1 1.0891
Chromatic Adaptation           : 1.04788 0.02292 -0.0502 0.02957 0.99049 -0.01706 -0.00923 0.01508 0.75165
Red Tone Reproduction Curve    : (Binary data 14 bytes, use -b option to extract)
Green Tone Reproduction Curve  : (Binary data 14 bytes, use -b option to extract)
Blue Tone Reproduction Curve   : (Binary data 14 bytes, use -b option to extract)
Profile Description            : Camera RGB Profile
Profile Copyright              : Copyright 2003 Apple Computer Inc., all rights reserved.
Profile Description ML         : Camera RGB Profile
Profile Description ML (es-ES) : Perfil RGB para Cámara
Profile Description ML (da-DK) : RGB-beskrivelse til Kamera
Profile Description ML (de-DE) : RGB-Profil für Kameras
Profile Description ML (fi-FI) : Kameran RGB-profiili
Profile Description ML (fr-FU) : Profil RVB de l'appareil-photo
Profile Description ML (it-IT) : Profilo RGB Fotocamera
Profile Description ML (nl-NL) : RGB-profiel Camera
Profile Description ML (no-NO) : RGB-kameraprofil
Profile Description ML (pt-BR) : Perfil RGB de Câmera
Profile Description ML (sv-SE) : RGB-profil för Kamera
Profile Description ML (ja-JP) : カメラ RGB プロファイル
Profile Description ML (ko-KR) : 카메라 RGB 프로파일
Profile Description ML (zh-TW) : 數位相機 RGB 色彩描述
```

```
Profile Description ML (zh-CN)   : 相机 RGB 描述文件
Aperture                         : 2.8
Image Size                       : 2592x1944
Megapixels                       : 5.0
Shutter Speed                    : 1/50
Thumbnail Image                  : (Binary data 3854 bytes, use -b option to extract)
Focal Length                     : 5.8 mm
Light Value                      : 8.3
```

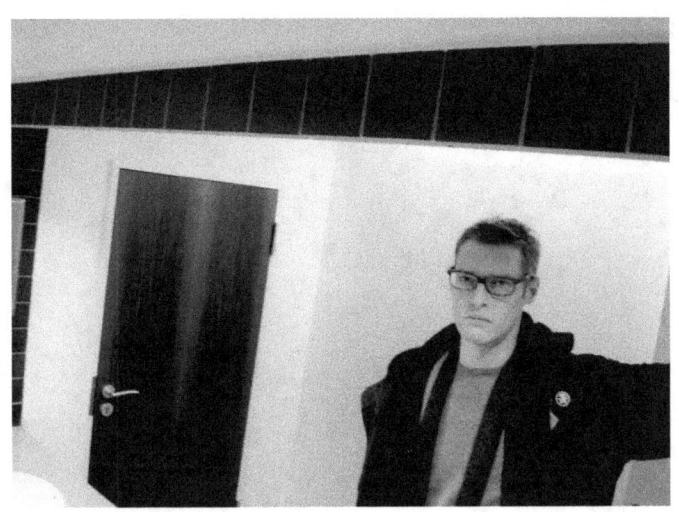

```
ExifTool Version Number         : 10.05
File Name                       : DSC00736.JPG
Directory                       : ../Selection
File Size                       : 1610 kB
File Modification Date/Time     : 2007:11:16 22:51:22+01:00
File Access Date/Time           : 2015:11:29 14:04:27+01:00
File Inode Change Date/Time     : 2015:11:05 21:35:08+01:00
File Permissions                : rw-r--r--
File Type                       : JPEG
File Type Extension             : jpg
MIME Type                       : image/jpeg
Exif Byte Order                 : Little-endian (Intel, II)
Image Description               :
Make                            : SONY
Camera Model Name               : DSC-W80
Orientation                     : Horizontal (normal)
X Resolution                    : 72
Y Resolution                    : 72
Resolution Unit                 : inches
Modify Date                     : 2007:11:15 18:12:43
Y Cb Cr Positioning             : Co-sited
Exposure Time                   : 1/30
F Number                        : 2.8
Exposure Program                : Program AE
ISO                             : 400
Exif Version                    : 0221
Date/Time Original              : 2007:11:15 18:12:43
Create Date                     : 2007:11:15 18:12:43
Components Configuration        : Y, Cb, Cr, -
Compressed Bits Per Pixel       : 4
Exposure Compensation           : 0
Max Aperture Value              : 2.8
Metering Mode                   : Multi-segment
Light Source                    : Unknown
Flash                           : Off, Did not fire
Focal Length                    : 5.8 mm
Creative Style                  : Standard
Macro                           : Off
Focus Mode                      : AF-C
AF Area Mode                    : Default
AF Illuminator                  : Auto
JPEG Quality                    : Standard
Flash Level                     : Normal
Release Mode                    : Normal
Sequence Number                 : Single
Anti-Blur                       : On (Shooting)
Flashpix Version                : 0100
Color Space                     : sRGB
Exif Image Width                : 2592
Exif Image Height               : 1944
Interoperability Index          : R98 - DCF basic file (sRGB)
Interoperability Version        : 0100
File Source                     : Digital Camera
Scene Type                      : Directly photographed
Custom Rendered                 : Normal
Exposure Mode                   : Auto
White Balance                   : Auto
Scene Capture Type              : Standard
Contrast                        : Normal
Saturation                      : Normal
Sharpness                       : Normal
PrintIM Version                 : 0300
Compression                     : JPEG (old-style)
Thumbnail Offset                : 9384
Thumbnail Length                : 9336
Profile CMM Type                : appl
Profile Version                 : 2.2.0
Profile Class                   : Input Device Profile
Color Space Data                : RGB
Profile Connection Space        : XYZ
Profile Date Time               : 2003:07:01 00:00:00
Profile File Signature          : acsp
Primary Platform                : Apple Computer Inc.
CMM Flags                       : Not Embedded, Independent
Device Manufacturer             : appl
Device Model                    :
Device Attributes               : Reflective, Glossy, Positive, Color
Rendering Intent                : Perceptual
Connection Space Illuminant     : 0.9642 1 0.82491
Profile Creator                 : appl
Profile ID                      : 0
Red Matrix Column               : 0.45427 0.24263 0.01482
Green Matrix Column             : 0.35332 0.67441 0.09042
Blue Matrix Column              : 0.15662 0.08336 0.71953
Media White Point               : 0.95047 1 1.0891
Chromatic Adaptation            : 1.04788 0.02292 -0.0502 0.02957 0.99049 -0.01706 -0.00923 0.01508 0.75165
```

```
Red Tone Reproduction Curve      : (Binary data 14 bytes, use -b option to extract)
Green Tone Reproduction Curve    : (Binary data 14 bytes, use -b option to extract)
Blue Tone Reproduction Curve     : (Binary data 14 bytes, use -b option to extract)
Profile Description              : Camera RGB Profile
Profile Copyright                : Copyright 2003 Apple Computer Inc., all rights reserved.
Profile Description ML           : Camera RGB Profile
Profile Description ML (es-ES)   : Perfil RGB para Cámara
Profile Description ML (da-DK)   : RGB-beskrivelse til Kamera
Profile Description ML (de-DE)   : RGB-Profil für Kameras
Profile Description ML (fi-FI)   : Kameran RGB-profiili
Profile Description ML (fr-FU)   : Profil RVB de l'appareil-photo
Profile Description ML (it-IT)   : Profilo RGB Fotocamera
Profile Description ML (nl-NL)   : RGB-profiel Camera
Profile Description ML (no-NO)   : RGB-kameraprofil
Profile Description ML (pt-BR)   : Perfil RGB de Câmera
Profile Description ML (sv-SE)   : RGB-profil för Kamera
Profile Description ML (ja-JP)   : カメラ RGB プロファイル
Profile Description ML (ko-KR)   : 카메라 RGB 프로파일
Profile Description ML (zh-TW)   : 數位相機 RGB 色彩描述
Profile Description ML (zh-CN)   : 相机 RGB 描述文件
Image Width                      : 2592
Image Height                     : 1944
Encoding Process                 : Baseline DCT, Huffman coding
Bits Per Sample                  : 8
Color Components                 : 3
Y Cb Cr Sub Sampling             : YCbCr4:2:2 (2 1)
Aperture                         : 2.8
Image Size                       : 2592x1944
Megapixels                       : 5.0
Shutter Speed                    : 1/30
Thumbnail Image                  : (Binary data 9336 bytes, use -b option to extract)
Focal Length                     : 5.8 mm
Light Value                      : 5.9
```

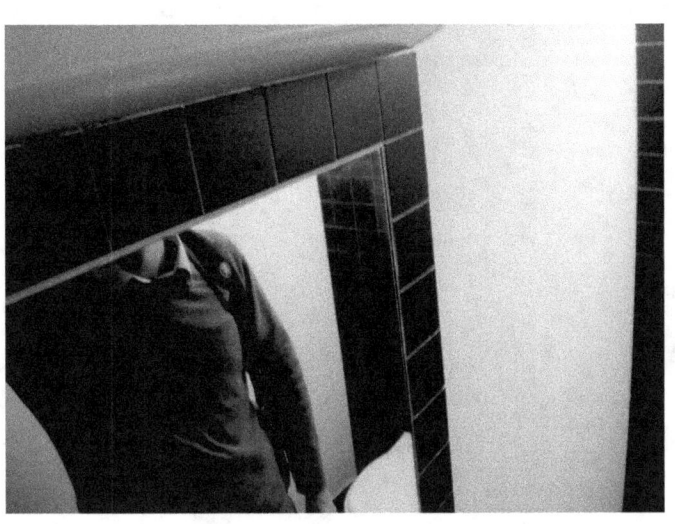

```
ExifTool Version Number         : 10.05
File Name                       : DSC00738.JPG
Directory                       : ../Selection
File Size                       : 1639 kB
File Modification Date/Time     : 2007:11:16 22:51:22+01:00
File Access Date/Time           : 2015:11:29 14:04:27+01:00
File Inode Change Date/Time     : 2015:11:05 21:35:08+01:00
File Permissions                : rw-r--r--
File Type                       : JPEG
File Type Extension             : jpg
MIME Type                       : image/jpeg
Exif Byte Order                 : Little-endian (Intel, II)
Image Description               :
Make                            : SONY
Camera Model Name               : DSC-W80
Orientation                     : Horizontal (normal)
X Resolution                    : 72
Y Resolution                    : 72
Resolution Unit                 : inches
Modify Date                     : 2007:11:16 15:15:31
Y Cb Cr Positioning             : Co-sited
Exposure Time                   : 1/13
F Number                        : 2.8
Exposure Program                : Program AE
ISO                             : 400
Exif Version                    : 0221
Date/Time Original              : 2007:11:16 15:15:31
Create Date                     : 2007:11:16 15:15:31
Components Configuration        : Y, Cb, Cr, -
Compressed Bits Per Pixel       : 4
Exposure Compensation           : 0
Max Aperture Value              : 2.8
Metering Mode                   : Multi-segment
Light Source                    : Unknown
Flash                           : Off, Did not fire
Focal Length                    : 5.8 mm
Creative Style                  : Standard
Macro                           : Off
Focus Mode                      : AF-C
AF Area Mode                    : Default
AF Illuminator                  : Auto
JPEG Quality                    : Standard
Flash Level                     : Normal
Release Mode                    : Normal
Sequence Number                 : Single
Anti-Blur                       : On (Shooting)
Flashpix Version                : 0100
Color Space                     : sRGB
Exif Image Width                : 2592
Exif Image Height               : 1944
Interoperability Index          : R98 - DCF basic file (sRGB)
Interoperability Version        : 0100
File Source                     : Digital Camera
Scene Type                      : Directly photographed
Custom Rendered                 : Normal
Exposure Mode                   : Auto
White Balance                   : Auto
Scene Capture Type              : Standard
Contrast                        : Normal
Saturation                      : Normal
Sharpness                       : Normal
PrintIM Version                 : 0300
Compression                     : JPEG (old-style)
Thumbnail Offset                : 9384
Thumbnail Length                : 7702
Profile CMM Type                : appl
Profile Version                 : 2.2.0
Profile Class                   : Input Device Profile
Color Space Data                : RGB
Profile Connection Space        : XYZ
Profile Date Time               : 2003:07:01 00:00:00
Profile File Signature          : acsp
Primary Platform                : Apple Computer Inc.
CMM Flags                       : Not Embedded, Independent
Device Manufacturer             : appl
Device Model                    :
Device Attributes               : Reflective, Glossy, Positive, Color
Rendering Intent                : Perceptual
Connection Space Illuminant     : 0.9642 1 0.82491
Profile Creator                 : appl
Profile ID                      : 0
Red Matrix Column               : 0.45427 0.24263 0.01482
Green Matrix Column             : 0.35332 0.67441 0.09042
Blue Matrix Column              : 0.15662 0.08336 0.71953
Media White Point               : 0.95047 1 1.0891
Chromatic Adaptation            : 1.04788 0.02292 -0.0502 0.02957 0.99049 -0.01706 -0.00923 0.01508 0.75165
```

```
Red Tone Reproduction Curve    : (Binary data 14 bytes, use -b option to extract)
Green Tone Reproduction Curve  : (Binary data 14 bytes, use -b option to extract)
Blue Tone Reproduction Curve   : (Binary data 14 bytes, use -b option to extract)
Profile Description            : Camera RGB Profile
Profile Copyright              : Copyright 2003 Apple Computer Inc., all rights reserved.
Profile Description ML         : Camera RGB Profile
Profile Description ML (es-ES) : Perfil RGB para Cámara
Profile Description ML (da-DK) : RGB-beskrivelse til Kamera
Profile Description ML (de-DE) : RGB-Profil für Kameras
Profile Description ML (fi-FI) : Kameran RGB-profiili
Profile Description ML (fr-FU) : Profil RVB de l'appareil-photo
Profile Description ML (it-IT) : Profilo RGB Fotocamera
Profile Description ML (nl-NL) : RGB-profiel Camera
Profile Description ML (no-NO) : RGB-kameraprofil
Profile Description ML (pt-BR) : Perfil RGB de Câmera
Profile Description ML (sv-SE) : RGB-profil för Kamera
Profile Description ML (ja-JP) : カメラ RGB プロファイル
Profile Description ML (ko-KR) : 카메라 RGB 프로파일
Profile Description ML (zh-TW) : 數位相機 RGB 色彩描述
Profile Description ML (zh-CN) : 相机 RGB 描述文件
Image Width                    : 2592
Image Height                   : 1944
Encoding Process               : Baseline DCT, Huffman coding
Bits Per Sample                : 8
Color Components               : 3
Y Cb Cr Sub Sampling           : YCbCr4:2:2 (2 1)
Aperture                       : 2.8
Image Size                     : 2592x1944
Megapixels                     : 5.0
Shutter Speed                  : 1/13
Thumbnail Image                : (Binary data 7702 bytes, use -b option to extract)
Focal Length                   : 5.8 mm
Light Value                    : 4.7
```

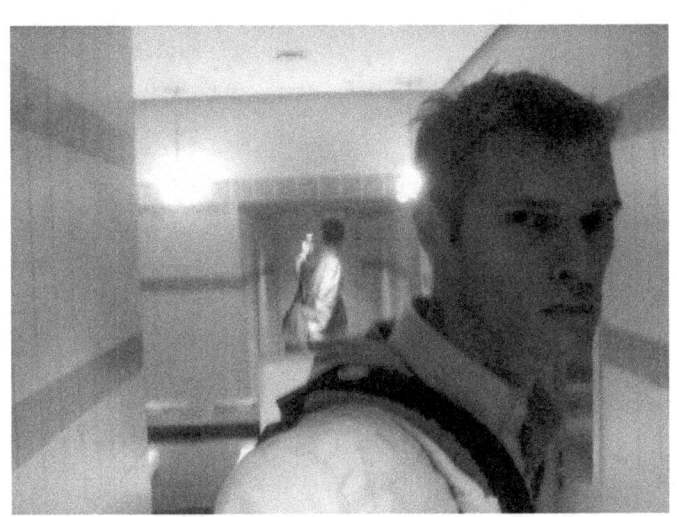

```
ExifTool Version Number         : 10.05
File Name                       : 070621_121318.jpg
Directory                       : ../Selection
File Size                       : 100 kB
File Modification Date/Time     : 2007:11:30 22:02:59+01:00
File Access Date/Time           : 2015:11:29 14:04:28+01:00
File Inode Change Date/Time     : 2015:11:05 21:35:08+01:00
File Permissions                : rw-r--r--
File Type                       : JPEG
File Type Extension             : jpg
MIME Type                       : image/jpeg
JFIF Version                    : 1.02
Resolution Unit                 : None
X Resolution                    : 1
Y Resolution                    : 1
Image Width                     : 1280
Image Height                    : 960
Encoding Process                : Baseline DCT, Huffman coding
Bits Per Sample                 : 8
Color Components                : 3
Y Cb Cr Sub Sampling            : YCbCr4:2:2 (2 1)
Image Size                      : 1280x960
Megapixels                      : 1.2
```

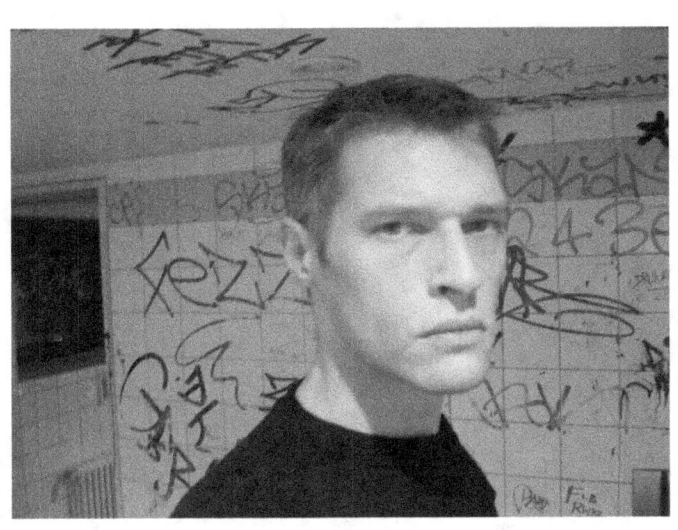

```
ExifTool Version Number         : 10.05
File Name                       : DSC00848.JPG
Directory                       : ../Selection
File Size                       : 1333 kB
File Modification Date/Time     : 2007:12:28 19:30:16+01:00
File Access Date/Time           : 2015:11:29 14:04:28+01:00
File Inode Change Date/Time     : 2015:11:05 21:35:08+01:00
File Permissions                : rw-r--r--
File Type                       : JPEG
File Type Extension             : jpg
MIME Type                       : image/jpeg
Exif Byte Order                 : Little-endian (Intel, II)
Image Description               :
Make                            : SONY
Camera Model Name               : DSC-W80
Orientation                     : Horizontal (normal)
X Resolution                    : 72
Y Resolution                    : 72
Resolution Unit                 : inches
Modify Date                     : 2007:12:27 23:15:35
Y Cb Cr Positioning             : Co-sited
Exposure Time                   : 1/15
F Number                        : 2.8
Exposure Program                : Program AE
ISO                             : 400
Exif Version                    : 0221
Date/Time Original              : 2007:12:27 23:15:35
Create Date                     : 2007:12:27 23:15:35
Components Configuration        : Y, Cb, Cr, -
Compressed Bits Per Pixel       : 4
Exposure Compensation           : 0
Max Aperture Value              : 2.8
Metering Mode                   : Multi-segment
Light Source                    : Unknown
Flash                           : Off, Did not fire
Focal Length                    : 5.8 mm
Creative Style                  : Standard
Macro                           : Off
Focus Mode                      : AF-S
AF Area Mode                    : Unknown (255)
AF Illuminator                  : Off
JPEG Quality                    : Standard
Flash Level                     : Normal
Release Mode                    : Continuous
Sequence Number                 : 2
Anti-Blur                       : On (Shooting)
Flashpix Version                : 0100
Color Space                     : sRGB
Exif Image Width                : 2592
Exif Image Height               : 1944
Interoperability Index          : R98 - DCF basic file (sRGB)
Interoperability Version        : 0100
File Source                     : Digital Camera
Scene Type                      : Directly photographed
Custom Rendered                 : Custom
Exposure Mode                   : Auto
White Balance                   : Auto
Scene Capture Type              : Standard
Contrast                        : Normal
Saturation                      : Normal
Sharpness                       : Normal
PrintIM Version                 : 0300
Compression                     : JPEG (old-style)
Thumbnail Offset                : 9384
Thumbnail Length                : 8653
Profile CMM Type                : appl
Profile Version                 : 2.2.0
Profile Class                   : Input Device Profile
Color Space Data                : RGB
Profile Connection Space        : XYZ
Profile Date Time               : 2003:07:01 00:00:00
Profile File Signature          : acsp
Primary Platform                : Apple Computer Inc.
CMM Flags                       : Not Embedded, Independent
Device Manufacturer             : appl
Device Model                    :
Device Attributes               : Reflective, Glossy, Positive, Color
Rendering Intent                : Perceptual
Connection Space Illuminant     : 0.9642 1 0.82491
Profile Creator                 : appl
Profile ID                      : 0
Red Matrix Column               : 0.45427 0.24263 0.01482
Green Matrix Column             : 0.35332 0.67441 0.09042
Blue Matrix Column              : 0.15662 0.08336 0.71953
Media White Point               : 0.95047 1 1.0891
Chromatic Adaptation            : 1.04788 0.02292 -0.0502 0.02957 0.99049 -0.01706 -0.00923 0.01508 0.75165
```

```
Red Tone Reproduction Curve     : (Binary data 14 bytes, use -b option to extract)
Green Tone Reproduction Curve   : (Binary data 14 bytes, use -b option to extract)
Blue Tone Reproduction Curve    : (Binary data 14 bytes, use -b option to extract)
Profile Description             : Camera RGB Profile
Profile Copyright               : Copyright 2003 Apple Computer Inc., all rights reserved.
Profile Description ML          : Camera RGB Profile
Profile Description ML (es-ES)  : Perfil RGB para Cámara
Profile Description ML (da-DK)  : RGB-beskrivelse til Kamera
Profile Description ML (de-DE)  : RGB-Profil für Kameras
Profile Description ML (fi-FI)  : Kameran RGB-profiili
Profile Description ML (fr-FU)  : Profil RVB de l'appareil-photo
Profile Description ML (it-IT)  : Profilo RGB Fotocamera
Profile Description ML (nl-NL)  : RGB-profiel Camera
Profile Description ML (no-NO)  : RGB-kameraprofil
Profile Description ML (pt-BR)  : Perfil RGB de Câmera
Profile Description ML (sv-SE)  : RGB-profil för Kamera
Profile Description ML (ja-JP)  : カメラ RGB プロファイル
Profile Description ML (ko-KR)  : 카메라 RGB 프로파일
Profile Description ML (zh-TW)  : 數位相機 RGB 色彩描述
Profile Description ML (zh-CN)  : 相机 RGB 描述文件
Image Width                     : 2592
Image Height                    : 1944
Encoding Process                : Baseline DCT, Huffman coding
Bits Per Sample                 : 8
Color Components                : 3
Y Cb Cr Sub Sampling            : YCbCr4:2:2 (2 1)
Aperture                        : 2.8
Image Size                      : 2592x1944
Megapixels                      : 5.0
Shutter Speed                   : 1/15
Thumbnail Image                 : (Binary data 8653 bytes, use -b option to extract)
Focal Length                    : 5.8 mm
Light Value                     : 4.9
```

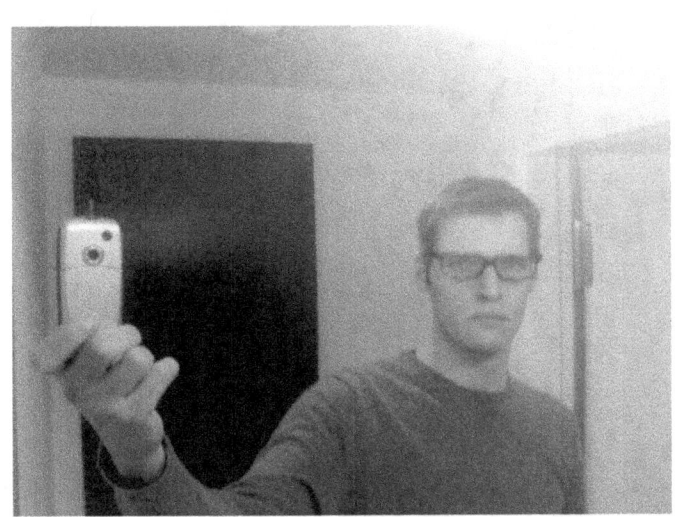

```
ExifTool Version Number         : 10.05
File Name                       : 071206_154942.jpg
Directory                       : ../Selection
File Size                       : 72 kB
File Modification Date/Time     : 2008:01:06 14:00:07+01:00
File Access Date/Time           : 2015:11:29 14:04:28+01:00
File Inode Change Date/Time     : 2015:11:05 21:35:08+01:00
File Permissions                : rw-r--r--
File Type                       : JPEG
File Type Extension             : jpg
MIME Type                       : image/jpeg
JFIF Version                    : 1.02
Resolution Unit                 : None
X Resolution                    : 1
Y Resolution                    : 1
Image Width                     : 1280
Image Height                    : 960
Encoding Process                : Baseline DCT, Huffman coding
Bits Per Sample                 : 8
Color Components                : 3
Y Cb Cr Sub Sampling            : YCbCr4:2:2 (2 1)
Image Size                      : 1280x960
Megapixels                      : 1.2
```

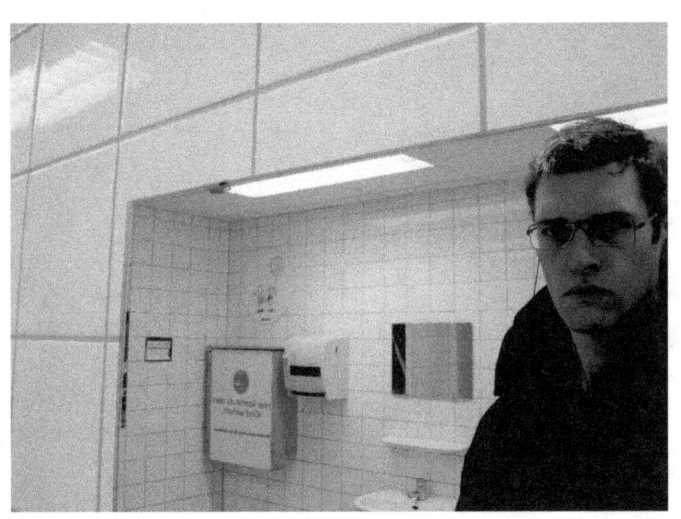

```
ExifTool Version Number         : 10.05
File Name                       : DSC00961.JPG
Directory                       : ../Selection
File Size                       : 1884 kB
File Modification Date/Time     : 2008:01:26 09:30:25+01:00
File Access Date/Time           : 2015:11:29 14:04:29+01:00
File Inode Change Date/Time     : 2015:11:05 21:35:08+01:00
File Permissions                : rw-r--r--
File Type                       : JPEG
File Type Extension             : jpg
MIME Type                       : image/jpeg
Exif Byte Order                 : Little-endian (Intel, II)
Image Description               :
Make                            : SONY
Camera Model Name               : DSC-W80
Orientation                     : Horizontal (normal)
X Resolution                    : 72
Y Resolution                    : 72
Resolution Unit                 : inches
Modify Date                     : 2008:01:22 16:26:55
Y Cb Cr Positioning             : Co-sited
Exposure Time                   : 1/100
F Number                        : 2.8
Exposure Program                : Program AE
ISO                             : 125
Exif Version                    : 0221
Date/Time Original              : 2008:01:22 16:26:55
Create Date                     : 2008:01:22 16:26:55
Components Configuration        : Y, Cb, Cr, -
Compressed Bits Per Pixel       : 4
Exposure Compensation           : 0
Max Aperture Value              : 2.8
Metering Mode                   : Multi-segment
Light Source                    : Unknown
Flash                           : Off, Did not fire
Focal Length                    : 5.8 mm
Creative Style                  : Standard
Macro                           : Off
Focus Mode                      : AF-S
AF Area Mode                    : Multi
AF Illuminator                  : Off
JPEG Quality                    : Standard
Flash Level                     : Normal
Release Mode                    : Continuous
Sequence Number                 : 1
Anti-Blur                       : On (Shooting)
Flashpix Version                : 0100
Color Space                     : sRGB
Exif Image Width                : 2592
Exif Image Height               : 1944
Interoperability Index          : R98 - DCF basic file (sRGB)
Interoperability Version        : 0100
File Source                     : Digital Camera
Scene Type                      : Directly photographed
Custom Rendered                 : Normal
Exposure Mode                   : Auto
White Balance                   : Auto
Scene Capture Type              : Standard
Contrast                        : Low
Saturation                      : Normal
Sharpness                       : Normal
PrintIM Version                 : 0300
Compression                     : JPEG (old-style)
Thumbnail Offset                : 9384
Thumbnail Length                : 8465
Profile CMM Type                : appl
Profile Version                 : 2.2.0
Profile Class                   : Input Device Profile
Color Space Data                : RGB
Profile Connection Space        : XYZ
Profile Date Time               : 2003:07:01 00:00:00
Profile File Signature          : acsp
Primary Platform                : Apple Computer Inc.
CMM Flags                       : Not Embedded, Independent
Device Manufacturer             : appl
Device Model                    :
Device Attributes               : Reflective, Glossy, Positive, Color
Rendering Intent                : Perceptual
Connection Space Illuminant     : 0.9642 1 0.82491
Profile Creator                 : appl
Profile ID                      : 0
Red Matrix Column               : 0.45427 0.24263 0.01482
Green Matrix Column             : 0.35332 0.67441 0.09042
Blue Matrix Column              : 0.15662 0.08336 0.71953
Media White Point               : 0.95047 1 1.0891
Chromatic Adaptation            : 1.04788 0.02292 -0.0502 0.02957 0.99049 -0.01706 -0.00923 0.01508 0.75165
```

```
Red Tone Reproduction Curve     : (Binary data 14 bytes, use -b option to extract)
Green Tone Reproduction Curve   : (Binary data 14 bytes, use -b option to extract)
Blue Tone Reproduction Curve    : (Binary data 14 bytes, use -b option to extract)
Profile Description             : Camera RGB Profile
Profile Copyright               : Copyright 2003 Apple Computer Inc., all rights reserved.
Profile Description ML          : Camera RGB Profile
Profile Description ML (es-ES)  : Perfil RGB para Cámara
Profile Description ML (da-DK)  : RGB-beskrivelse til Kamera
Profile Description ML (de-DE)  : RGB-Profil für Kameras
Profile Description ML (fi-FI)  : Kameran RGB-profiili
Profile Description ML (fr-FU)  : Profil RVB de l'appareil-photo
Profile Description ML (it-IT)  : Profilo RGB Fotocamera
Profile Description ML (nl-NL)  : RGB-profiel Camera
Profile Description ML (no-NO)  : RGB-kameraprofil
Profile Description ML (pt-BR)  : Perfil RGB de Câmera
Profile Description ML (sv-SE)  : RGB-profil för Kamera
Profile Description ML (ja-JP)  : カメラ RGB プロファイル
Profile Description ML (ko-KR)  : 카메라 RGB 프로파일
Profile Description ML (zh-TW)  : 數位相機 RGB 色彩描述
Profile Description ML (zh-CN)  : 相机 RGB 描述文件
Image Width                     : 2592
Image Height                    : 1944
Encoding Process                : Baseline DCT, Huffman coding
Bits Per Sample                 : 8
Color Components                : 3
Y Cb Cr Sub Sampling            : YCbCr4:2:2 (2 1)
Aperture                        : 2.8
Image Size                      : 2592x1944
Megapixels                      : 5.0
Shutter Speed                   : 1/100
Thumbnail Image                 : (Binary data 8465 bytes, use -b option to extract)
Focal Length                    : 5.8 mm
Light Value                     : 9.3
```

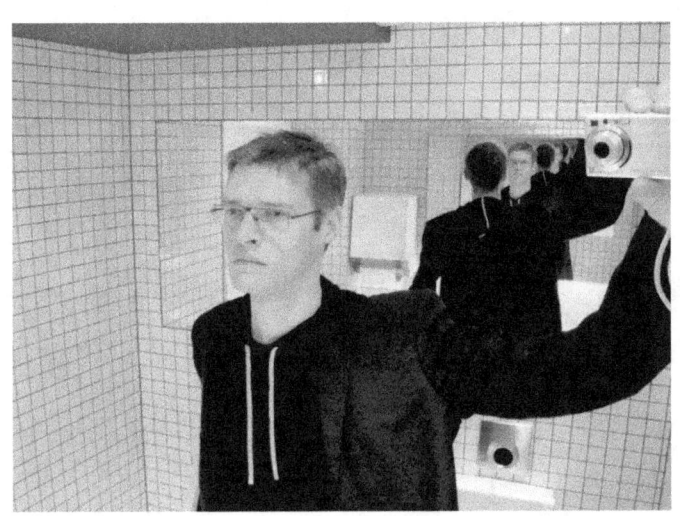

```
ExifTool Version Number         : 10.05
File Name                       : DSC01116.JPG
Directory                       : ../Selection
File Size                       : 1944 kB
File Modification Date/Time     : 2008:02:24 20:40:21+01:00
File Access Date/Time           : 2015:11:29 14:04:29+01:00
File Inode Change Date/Time     : 2015:11:05 21:35:08+01:00
File Permissions                : rw-r--r--
File Type                       : JPEG
File Type Extension             : jpg
MIME Type                       : image/jpeg
Exif Byte Order                 : Little-endian (Intel, II)
Image Description               :
Make                            : SONY
Camera Model Name               : DSC-W80
Orientation                     : Horizontal (normal)
X Resolution                    : 72
Y Resolution                    : 72
Resolution Unit                 : inches
Modify Date                     : 2008:02:21 22:47:03
Y Cb Cr Positioning             : Co-sited
Exposure Time                   : 1/80
F Number                        : 2.8
Exposure Program                : Program AE
ISO                             : 1600
Exif Version                    : 0221
Date/Time Original              : 2008:02:21 22:47:03
Create Date                     : 2008:02:21 22:47:03
Components Configuration        : Y, Cb, Cr, -
Compressed Bits Per Pixel       : 4
Exposure Compensation           : 0
Max Aperture Value              : 2.8
Metering Mode                   : Multi-segment
Light Source                    : Unknown
Flash                           : Off, Did not fire
Focal Length                    : 5.8 mm
Creative Style                  : Standard
Macro                           : Off
Focus Mode                      : AF-S
AF Area Mode                    : Default
AF Illuminator                  : Off
JPEG Quality                    : Standard
Flash Level                     : Normal
Release Mode                    : Normal
Sequence Number                 : Single
Anti-Blur                       : On (Shooting)
Flashpix Version                : 0100
Color Space                     : sRGB
Exif Image Width                : 2592
Exif Image Height               : 1944
Interoperability Index          : R98 - DCF basic file (sRGB)
Interoperability Version        : 0100
File Source                     : Digital Camera
Scene Type                      : Directly photographed
Custom Rendered                 : Normal
Exposure Mode                   : Auto
White Balance                   : Auto
Scene Capture Type              : Standard
Contrast                        : Normal
Saturation                      : Normal
Sharpness                       : Normal
PrintIM Version                 : 0300
Compression                     : JPEG (old-style)
Thumbnail Offset                : 9384
Thumbnail Length                : 11517
Profile CMM Type                : appl
Profile Version                 : 2.2.0
Profile Class                   : Input Device Profile
Color Space Data                : RGB
Profile Connection Space        : XYZ
Profile Date Time               : 2003:07:01 00:00:00
Profile File Signature          : acsp
Primary Platform                : Apple Computer Inc.
CMM Flags                       : Not Embedded, Independent
Device Manufacturer             : appl
Device Model                    :
Device Attributes               : Reflective, Glossy, Positive, Color
Rendering Intent                : Perceptual
Connection Space Illuminant     : 0.9642 1 0.82491
Profile Creator                 : appl
Profile ID                      : 0
Red Matrix Column               : 0.45427 0.24263 0.01482
Green Matrix Column             : 0.35332 0.67441 0.09042
Blue Matrix Column              : 0.15662 0.08336 0.71953
Media White Point               : 0.95047 1 1.0891
Chromatic Adaptation            : 1.04788 0.02292 -0.0502 0.02957 0.99049 -0.01706 -0.00923 0.01508 0.75165
```

```
Red Tone Reproduction Curve     : (Binary data 14 bytes, use -b option to extract)
Green Tone Reproduction Curve   : (Binary data 14 bytes, use -b option to extract)
Blue Tone Reproduction Curve    : (Binary data 14 bytes, use -b option to extract)
Profile Description             : Camera RGB Profile
Profile Copyright               : Copyright 2003 Apple Computer Inc., all rights reserved.
Profile Description ML          : Camera RGB Profile
Profile Description ML (es-ES)  : Perfil RGB para Cámara
Profile Description ML (da-DK)  : RGB-beskrivelse til Kamera
Profile Description ML (de-DE)  : RGB-Profil für Kameras
Profile Description ML (fi-FI)  : Kameran RGB-profiili
Profile Description ML (fr-FU)  : Profil RVB de l'appareil-photo
Profile Description ML (it-IT)  : Profilo RGB Fotocamera
Profile Description ML (nl-NL)  : RGB-profiel Camera
Profile Description ML (no-NO)  : RGB-kameraprofil
Profile Description ML (pt-BR)  : Perfil RGB de Câmera
Profile Description ML (sv-SE)  : RGB-profil för Kamera
Profile Description ML (ja-JP)  : カメラ RGB プロファイル
Profile Description ML (ko-KR)  : 카메라 RGB 프로파일
Profile Description ML (zh-TW)  : 數位相機 RGB 色彩描述
Profile Description ML (zh-CN)  : 相机 RGB 描述文件
Image Width                     : 2592
Image Height                    : 1944
Encoding Process                : Baseline DCT, Huffman coding
Bits Per Sample                 : 8
Color Components                : 3
Y Cb Cr Sub Sampling            : YCbCr4:2:2 (2 1)
Aperture                        : 2.8
Image Size                      : 2592x1944
Megapixels                      : 5.0
Shutter Speed                   : 1/80
Thumbnail Image                 : (Binary data 11517 bytes, use -b option to extract)
Focal Length                    : 5.8 mm
Light Value                     : 5.3
```

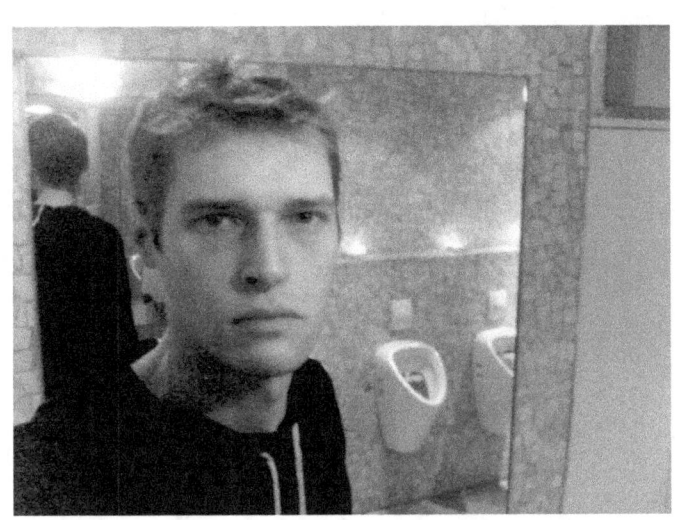

```
ExifTool Version Number         : 10.05
File Name                       : 080222_180427.jpg
Directory                       : ../Selection
File Size                       : 287 kB
Resource Fork Size              : 56 kB
File Modification Date/Time     : 2008:02:22 21:12:38+01:00
File Access Date/Time           : 2015:11:29 14:04:30+01:00
File Inode Change Date/Time     : 2015:11:05 21:35:08+01:00
File Permissions                : rw-r--r--
File Type                       : JPEG
File Type Extension             : jpg
MIME Type                       : image/jpeg
JFIF Version                    : 1.02
Exif Byte Order                 : Big-endian (Motorola, MM)
Orientation                     : Horizontal (normal)
X Resolution                    : 72
Y Resolution                    : 72
Resolution Unit                 : inches
Software                        : Adobe Photoshop CS3 Macintosh
Modify Date                     : 2008:02:22 21:12:35
Color Space                     : Uncalibrated
Exif Image Width                : 1280
Exif Image Height               : 960
Compression                     : JPEG (old-style)
Thumbnail Offset                : 332
Thumbnail Length                : 4376
Current IPTC Digest             : e8f15cf32fc118a1a27b67adc564d5ba
Application Record Version      : 0
IPTC Digest                     : e8f15cf32fc118a1a27b67adc564d5ba
Displayed Units X               : inches
Displayed Units Y               : inches
Global Angle                    : 30
Global Altitude                 : 30
Copyright Flag                  : False
Photoshop Thumbnail             : (Binary data 4376 bytes, use -b option to extract)
Photoshop Quality               : 10
Photoshop Format                : Standard
Progressive Scans               : 3 Scans
XMP Toolkit                     : Adobe XMP Core 4.1-c036 46.276720, Mon Feb 19 2007 22:13:43
Create Date                     : 2008:02:22 21:09:41+01:00
Metadata Date                   : 2008:02:22 21:12:35+01:00
Creator Tool                    : Adobe Photoshop CS3 Macintosh
Format                          : image/jpeg
Color Mode                      : RGB
History                         :
Instance ID                     : uuid:FF4A740B1DE3DC11B87A9DA628CFEF0D
Native Digest                   : 256,257,258,259,262,274,277,284,530,531,282,283,296,301,318,319,529,532,306,270,271,272,305,315,33432;2638CCC2E8
DCT Encode Version              : 100
APP14 Flags 0                   : [14]
APP14 Flags 1                   : (none)
Color Transform                 : YCbCr
Image Width                     : 1280
Image Height                    : 960
Encoding Process                : Baseline DCT, Huffman coding
Bits Per Sample                 : 8
Color Components                : 3
Y Cb Cr Sub Sampling            : YCbCr4:4:4 (1 1)
Image Size                      : 1280x960
Megapixels                      : 1.2
Thumbnail Image                 : (Binary data 4376 bytes, use -b option to extract)
```

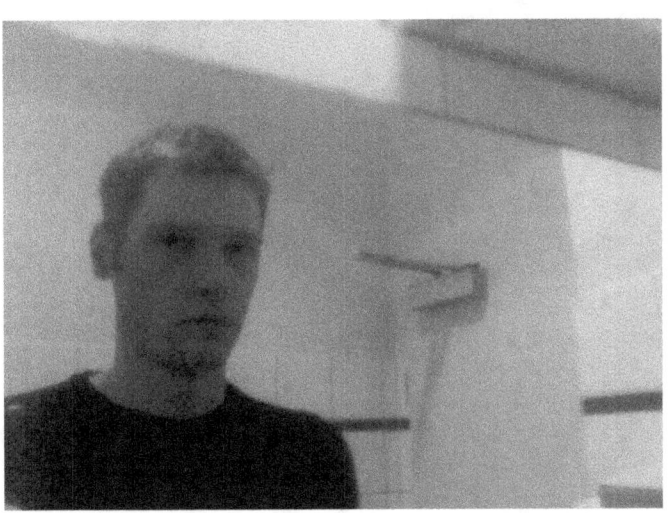

```
ExifTool Version Number         : 10.05
File Name                       : 080201_222925.jpg
Directory                       : ../Selection
File Size                       : 74 kB
File Modification Date/Time     : 2008:02:22 21:16:31+01:00
File Access Date/Time           : 2015:11:29 14:04:30+01:00
File Inode Change Date/Time     : 2015:11:05 21:35:08+01:00
File Permissions                : rw-r--r--
File Type                       : JPEG
File Type Extension             : jpg
MIME Type                       : image/jpeg
JFIF Version                    : 1.02
Resolution Unit                 : None
X Resolution                    : 1
Y Resolution                    : 1
Image Width                     : 1280
Image Height                    : 960
Encoding Process                : Baseline DCT, Huffman coding
Bits Per Sample                 : 8
Color Components                : 3
Y Cb Cr Sub Sampling            : YCbCr4:2:2 (2 1)
Image Size                      : 1280x960
Megapixels                      : 1.2
```

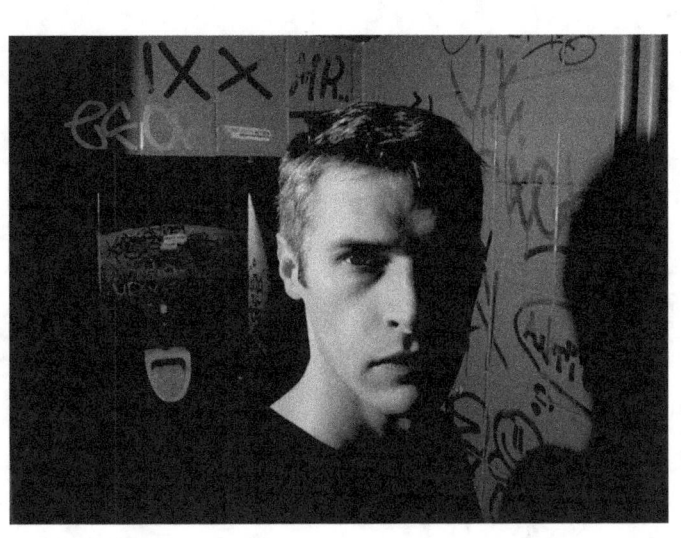

```
ExifTool Version Number         : 10.05
File Name                       : DSC01170.JPG
Directory                       : ../Selection
File Size                       : 1688 kB
File Modification Date/Time     : 2008:03:25 11:16:50+01:00
File Access Date/Time           : 2015:11:29 14:04:30+01:00
File Inode Change Date/Time     : 2015:11:05 21:35:08+01:00
File Permissions                : rw-r--r--
File Type                       : JPEG
File Type Extension             : jpg
MIME Type                       : image/jpeg
Exif Byte Order                 : Little-endian (Intel, II)
Image Description               :
Make                            : SONY
Camera Model Name               : DSC-W80
Orientation                     : Horizontal (normal)
X Resolution                    : 72
Y Resolution                    : 72
Resolution Unit                 : inches
Modify Date                     : 2008:03:24 03:06:39
Y Cb Cr Positioning             : Co-sited
Exposure Time                   : 1/20
F Number                        : 2.8
Exposure Program                : Program AE
ISO                             : 400
Exif Version                    : 0221
Date/Time Original              : 2008:03:24 03:06:39
Create Date                     : 2008:03:24 03:06:39
Components Configuration        : Y, Cb, Cr, -
Compressed Bits Per Pixel       : 4
Exposure Compensation           : 0
Max Aperture Value              : 2.8
Metering Mode                   : Multi-segment
Light Source                    : Unknown
Flash                           : Off, Did not fire
Focal Length                    : 5.8 mm
Creative Style                  : Standard
Macro                           : Off
Focus Mode                      : AF-C
AF Area Mode                    : Default
AF Illuminator                  : Off
JPEG Quality                    : Standard
Flash Level                     : Normal
Release Mode                    : Normal
Sequence Number                 : Single
Anti-Blur                       : On (Shooting)
Flashpix Version                : 0100
Color Space                     : sRGB
Exif Image Width                : 2592
Exif Image Height               : 1944
Interoperability Index          : R98 - DCF basic file (sRGB)
Interoperability Version        : 0100
File Source                     : Digital Camera
Scene Type                      : Directly photographed
Custom Rendered                 : Normal
Exposure Mode                   : Auto
White Balance                   : Auto
Scene Capture Type              : Standard
Contrast                        : Normal
Saturation                      : Normal
Sharpness                       : Normal
PrintIM Version                 : 0300
Compression                     : JPEG (old-style)
Thumbnail Offset                : 9384
Thumbnail Length                : 9798
Profile CMM Type                : appl
Profile Version                 : 2.2.0
Profile Class                   : Input Device Profile
Color Space Data                : RGB
Profile Connection Space        : XYZ
Profile Date Time               : 2003:07:01 00:00:00
Profile File Signature          : acsp
Primary Platform                : Apple Computer Inc.
CMM Flags                       : Not Embedded, Independent
Device Manufacturer             : appl
Device Model                    :
Device Attributes               : Reflective, Glossy, Positive, Color
Rendering Intent                : Perceptual
Connection Space Illuminant     : 0.9642 1 0.82491
Profile Creator                 : appl
Profile ID                      : 0
Red Matrix Column               : 0.45427 0.24263 0.01482
Green Matrix Column             : 0.35332 0.67441 0.09042
Blue Matrix Column              : 0.15662 0.08336 0.71953
Media White Point               : 0.95047 1 1.0891
Chromatic Adaptation            : 1.04788 0.02292 -0.0502 0.02957 0.99049 -0.01706 -0.00923 0.01508 0.75165
```

```
Red Tone Reproduction Curve        : (Binary data 14 bytes, use -b option to extract)
Green Tone Reproduction Curve      : (Binary data 14 bytes, use -b option to extract)
Blue Tone Reproduction Curve       : (Binary data 14 bytes, use -b option to extract)
Profile Description                : Camera RGB Profile
Profile Copyright                  : Copyright 2003 Apple Computer Inc., all rights reserved.
Profile Description ML             : Camera RGB Profile
Profile Description ML (es-ES)     : Perfil RGB para Cámara
Profile Description ML (da-DK)     : RGB-beskrivelse til Kamera
Profile Description ML (de-DE)     : RGB-Profil für Kameras
Profile Description ML (fi-FI)     : Kameran RGB-profiili
Profile Description ML (fr-FU)     : Profil RVB de l'appareil-photo
Profile Description ML (it-IT)     : Profilo RGB Fotocamera
Profile Description ML (nl-NL)     : RGB-profiel Camera
Profile Description ML (no-NO)     : RGB-kameraprofil
Profile Description ML (pt-BR)     : Perfil RGB de Câmera
Profile Description ML (sv-SE)     : RGB-profil för Kamera
Profile Description ML (ja-JP)     : カメラ RGB プロファイル
Profile Description ML (ko-KR)     : 카메라 RGB 프로파일
Profile Description ML (zh-TW)     : 數位相機 RGB 色彩描述
Profile Description ML (zh-CN)     : 相机 RGB 描述文件
Image Width                        : 2592
Image Height                       : 1944
Encoding Process                   : Baseline DCT, Huffman coding
Bits Per Sample                    : 8
Color Components                   : 3
Y Cb Cr Sub Sampling               : YCbCr4:2:2 (2 1)
Aperture                           : 2.8
Image Size                         : 2592x1944
Megapixels                         : 5.0
Shutter Speed                      : 1/20
Thumbnail Image                    : (Binary data 9798 bytes, use -b option to extract)
Focal Length                       : 5.8 mm
Light Value                        : 5.3
```

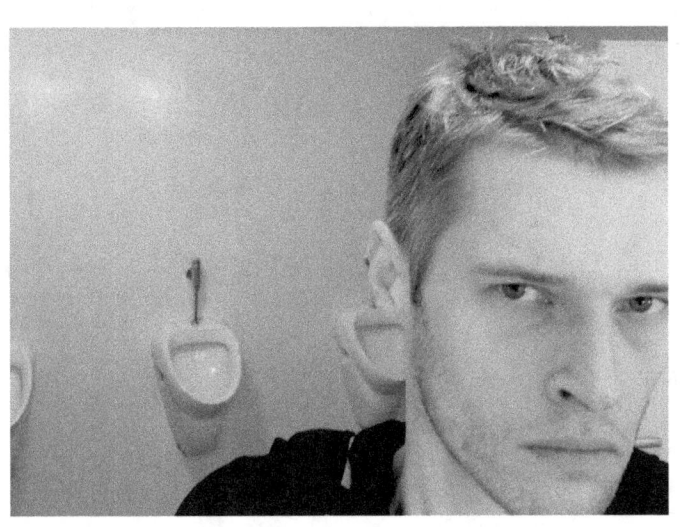

```
ExifTool Version Number         : 10.05
File Name                       : DSC01189.JPG
Directory                       : ../Selection
File Size                       : 2013 kB
File Modification Date/Time     : 2008:04:13 17:14:26+02:00
File Access Date/Time           : 2015:11:29 14:04:31+01:00
File Inode Change Date/Time     : 2015:11:05 21:35:08+01:00
File Permissions                : rw-r--r--
File Type                       : JPEG
File Type Extension             : jpg
MIME Type                       : image/jpeg
Exif Byte Order                 : Little-endian (Intel, II)
Image Description               :
Make                            : SONY
Camera Model Name               : DSC-W80
Orientation                     : Horizontal (normal)
X Resolution                    : 72
Y Resolution                    : 72
Resolution Unit                 : inches
Modify Date                     : 2008:04:11 20:09:42
Y Cb Cr Positioning             : Co-sited
Exposure Time                   : 1/10
F Number                        : 3.5
Exposure Program                : Program AE
ISO                             : 400
Exif Version                    : 0221
Date/Time Original              : 2008:04:11 20:09:42
Create Date                     : 2008:04:11 20:09:42
Components Configuration        : Y, Cb, Cr, -
Compressed Bits Per Pixel       : 4
Exposure Compensation           : 0
Max Aperture Value              : 2.8
Metering Mode                   : Multi-segment
Light Source                    : Unknown
Flash                           : Off, Did not fire
Focal Length                    : 8.7 mm
Creative Style                  : Standard
Macro                           : Off
Focus Mode                      : AF-S
AF Area Mode                    : Multi
AF Illuminator                  : Off
JPEG Quality                    : Standard
Flash Level                     : Normal
Release Mode                    : Normal
Sequence Number                 : Single
Anti-Blur                       : On (Shooting)
Flashpix Version                : 0100
Color Space                     : sRGB
Exif Image Width                : 2592
Exif Image Height               : 1944
Interoperability Index          : R98 - DCF basic file (sRGB)
Interoperability Version        : 0100
File Source                     : Digital Camera
Scene Type                      : Directly photographed
Custom Rendered                 : Normal
Exposure Mode                   : Auto
White Balance                   : Auto
Scene Capture Type              : Standard
Contrast                        : Normal
Saturation                      : Normal
Sharpness                       : Normal
PrintIM Version                 : 0300
Compression                     : JPEG (old-style)
Thumbnail Offset                : 9384
Thumbnail Length                : 8163
Profile CMM Type                : appl
Profile Version                 : 2.2.0
Profile Class                   : Input Device Profile
Color Space Data                : RGB
Profile Connection Space        : XYZ
Profile Date Time               : 2003:07:01 00:00:00
Profile File Signature          : acsp
Primary Platform                : Apple Computer Inc.
CMM Flags                       : Not Embedded, Independent
Device Manufacturer             : appl
Device Model                    :
Device Attributes               : Reflective, Glossy, Positive, Color
Rendering Intent                : Perceptual
Connection Space Illuminant     : 0.9642 1 0.82491
Profile Creator                 : appl
Profile ID                      : 0
Red Matrix Column               : 0.45427 0.24263 0.01482
Green Matrix Column             : 0.35332 0.67441 0.09042
Blue Matrix Column              : 0.15662 0.08336 0.71953
Media White Point               : 0.95047 1 1.0891
Chromatic Adaptation            : 1.04788 0.02292 -0.0502 0.02957 0.99049 -0.01706 -0.00923 0.01508 0.75165
```

```
Red Tone Reproduction Curve     : (Binary data 14 bytes, use -b option to extract)
Green Tone Reproduction Curve   : (Binary data 14 bytes, use -b option to extract)
Blue Tone Reproduction Curve    : (Binary data 14 bytes, use -b option to extract)
Profile Description             : Camera RGB Profile
Profile Copyright               : Copyright 2003 Apple Computer Inc., all rights reserved.
Profile Description ML          : Camera RGB Profile
Profile Description ML (es-ES)  : Perfil RGB para Cámara
Profile Description ML (da-DK)  : RGB-beskrivelse til Kamera
Profile Description ML (de-DE)  : RGB-Profil für Kameras
Profile Description ML (fi-FI)  : Kameran RGB-profiili
Profile Description ML (fr-FU)  : Profil RVB de l'appareil-photo
Profile Description ML (it-IT)  : Profilo RGB Fotocamera
Profile Description ML (nl-NL)  : RGB-profiel Camera
Profile Description ML (no-NO)  : RGB-kameraprofil
Profile Description ML (pt-BR)  : Perfil RGB de Câmera
Profile Description ML (sv-SE)  : RGB-profil för Kamera
Profile Description ML (ja-JP)  : カメラ RGB プロファイル
Profile Description ML (ko-KR)  : 카메라 RGB 프로파일
Profile Description ML (zh-TW)  : 數位相機 RGB 色彩描述
Profile Description ML (zh-CN)  : 相机 RGB 描述文件
Image Width                     : 2592
Image Height                    : 1944
Encoding Process                : Baseline DCT, Huffman coding
Bits Per Sample                 : 8
Color Components                : 3
Y Cb Cr Sub Sampling            : YCbCr4:2:2 (2 1)
Aperture                        : 3.5
Image Size                      : 2592x1944
Megapixels                      : 5.0
Shutter Speed                   : 1/10
Thumbnail Image                 : (Binary data 8163 bytes, use -b option to extract)
Focal Length                    : 8.7 mm
Light Value                     : 4.9
```

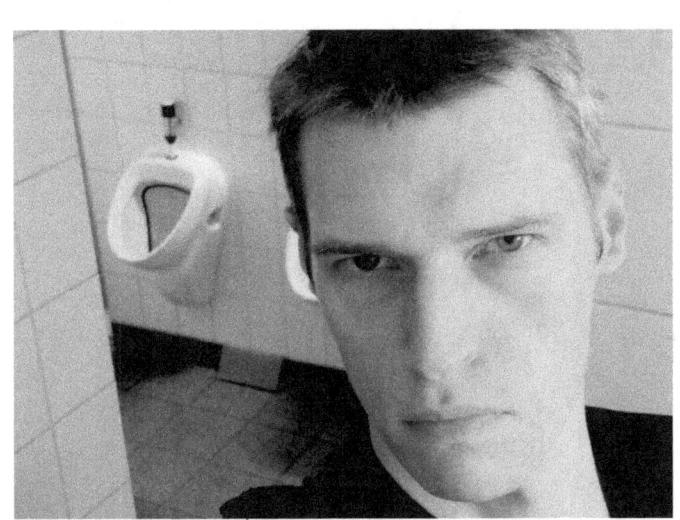

```
ExifTool Version Number        : 10.05
File Name                      : DSC01216.JPG
Directory                      : ../Selection
File Size                      : 1778 kB
File Modification Date/Time    : 2008:05:10 08:42:54+02:00
File Access Date/Time          : 2015:11:29 14:04:31+01:00
File Inode Change Date/Time    : 2015:11:05 21:35:08+01:00
File Permissions               : rw-r--r--
File Type                      : JPEG
File Type Extension            : jpg
MIME Type                      : image/jpeg
Exif Byte Order                : Little-endian (Intel, II)
Image Description              :
Make                           : SONY
Camera Model Name              : DSC-W80
Orientation                    : Horizontal (normal)
X Resolution                   : 72
Y Resolution                   : 72
Resolution Unit                : inches
Modify Date                    : 2008:04:27 23:08:05
Y Cb Cr Positioning            : Co-sited
Exposure Time                  : 1/15
F Number                       : 3.5
Exposure Program               : Program AE
ISO                            : 400
Exif Version                   : 0221
Date/Time Original             : 2008:04:27 23:08:05
Create Date                    : 2008:04:27 23:08:05
Components Configuration       : Y, Cb, Cr, -
Compressed Bits Per Pixel      : 4
Exposure Compensation          : 0
Max Aperture Value             : 2.8
Metering Mode                  : Multi-segment
Light Source                   : Unknown
Flash                          : Off, Did not fire
Focal Length                   : 10.0 mm
Creative Style                 : Standard
Macro                          : Off
Focus Mode                     : AF-S
AF Area Mode                   : Multi
AF Illuminator                 : Off
JPEG Quality                   : Standard
Flash Level                    : Normal
Release Mode                   : Normal
Sequence Number                : Single
Anti-Blur                      : On (Shooting)
Flashpix Version               : 0100
Color Space                    : sRGB
Exif Image Width               : 2592
Exif Image Height              : 1944
Interoperability Index         : R98 - DCF basic file (sRGB)
Interoperability Version       : 0100
File Source                    : Digital Camera
Scene Type                     : Directly photographed
Custom Rendered                : Normal
Exposure Mode                  : Auto
White Balance                  : Auto
Scene Capture Type             : Standard
Contrast                       : Normal
Saturation                     : Normal
Sharpness                      : Normal
PrintIM Version                : 0300
Compression                    : JPEG (old-style)
Thumbnail Offset               : 9384
Thumbnail Length               : 9950
Profile CMM Type               : appl
Profile Version                : 2.2.0
Profile Class                  : Input Device Profile
Color Space Data               : RGB
Profile Connection Space       : XYZ
Profile Date Time              : 2003:07:01 00:00:00
Profile File Signature         : acsp
Primary Platform               : Apple Computer Inc.
CMM Flags                      : Not Embedded, Independent
Device Manufacturer            : appl
Device Model                   :
Device Attributes              : Reflective, Glossy, Positive, Color
Rendering Intent               : Perceptual
Connection Space Illuminant    : 0.9642 1 0.82491
Profile Creator                : appl
Profile ID                     : 0
Red Matrix Column              : 0.45427 0.24263 0.01482
Green Matrix Column            : 0.35332 0.67441 0.09042
Blue Matrix Column             : 0.15662 0.08336 0.71953
Media White Point              : 0.95047 1 1.0891
Chromatic Adaptation           : 1.04788 0.02292 -0.0502 0.02957 0.99049 -0.01706 -0.00923 0.01508 0.75165
```

```
Red Tone Reproduction Curve     : (Binary data 14 bytes, use -b option to extract)
Green Tone Reproduction Curve   : (Binary data 14 bytes, use -b option to extract)
Blue Tone Reproduction Curve    : (Binary data 14 bytes, use -b option to extract)
Profile Description             : Camera RGB Profile
Profile Copyright               : Copyright 2003 Apple Computer Inc., all rights reserved.
Profile Description ML          : Camera RGB Profile
Profile Description ML (es-ES)  : Perfil RGB para Cámara
Profile Description ML (da-DK)  : RGB-beskrivelse til Kamera
Profile Description ML (de-DE)  : RGB-Profil für Kameras
Profile Description ML (fi-FI)  : Kameran RGB-profiili
Profile Description ML (fr-FU)  : Profil RVB de l'appareil-photo
Profile Description ML (it-IT)  : Profilo RGB Fotocamera
Profile Description ML (nl-NL)  : RGB-profiel Camera
Profile Description ML (no-NO)  : RGB-kameraprofil
Profile Description ML (pt-BR)  : Perfil RGB de Câmera
Profile Description ML (sv-SE)  : RGB-profil för Kamera
Profile Description ML (ja-JP)  : カメラ RGB プロファイル
Profile Description ML (ko-KR)  : 카메라 RGB 프로파일
Profile Description ML (zh-TW)  : 數位相機 RGB 色彩描述
Profile Description ML (zh-CN)  : 相机 RGB 描述文件
Image Width                     : 2592
Image Height                    : 1944
Encoding Process                : Baseline DCT, Huffman coding
Bits Per Sample                 : 8
Color Components                : 3
Y Cb Cr Sub Sampling            : YCbCr4:2:2 (2 1)
Aperture                        : 3.5
Image Size                      : 2592x1944
Megapixels                      : 5.0
Shutter Speed                   : 1/15
Thumbnail Image                 : (Binary data 9950 bytes, use -b option to extract)
Focal Length                    : 10.0 mm
Light Value                     : 5.5
```

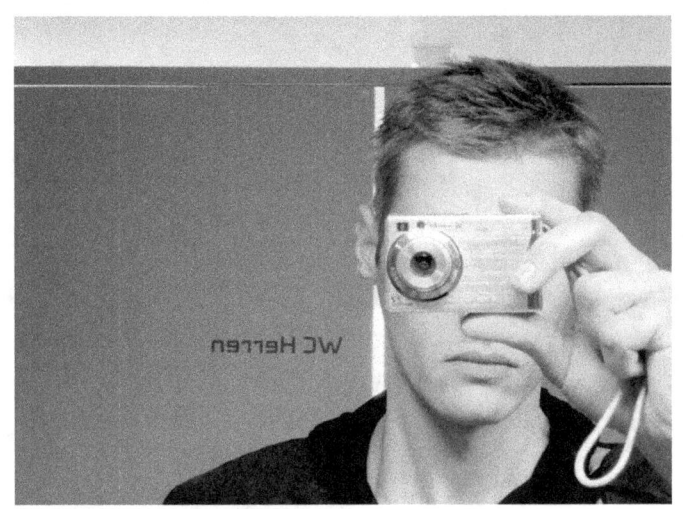

```
ExifTool Version Number         : 10.05
File Name                       : DSC01591.JPG
Directory                       : ../Selection
File Size                       : 1750 kB
File Modification Date/Time     : 2008:05:24 12:40:51+02:00
File Access Date/Time           : 2015:11:29 14:04:32+01:00
File Inode Change Date/Time     : 2015:11:05 21:35:08+01:00
File Permissions                : rw-r--r--
File Type                       : JPEG
File Type Extension             : jpg
MIME Type                       : image/jpeg
Exif Byte Order                 : Little-endian (Intel, II)
Image Description               :
Make                            : SONY
Camera Model Name               : DSC-W80
Orientation                     : Horizontal (normal)
X Resolution                    : 72
Y Resolution                    : 72
Resolution Unit                 : inches
Modify Date                     : 2008:05:20 13:44:32
Y Cb Cr Positioning             : Co-sited
Exposure Time                   : 1/13
F Number                        : 5.0
Exposure Program                : Program AE
ISO                             : 400
Exif Version                    : 0221
Date/Time Original              : 2008:05:20 13:44:32
Create Date                     : 2008:05:20 13:44:32
Components Configuration        : Y, Cb, Cr, -
Compressed Bits Per Pixel       : 4
Exposure Compensation           : 0
Max Aperture Value              : 2.8
Metering Mode                   : Multi-segment
Light Source                    : Unknown
Flash                           : Off, Did not fire
Focal Length                    : 15.1 mm
Creative Style                  : Standard
Macro                           : Off
Focus Mode                      : AF-C
AF Area Mode                    : Default
AF Illuminator                  : Off
JPEG Quality                    : Standard
Flash Level                     : Normal
Release Mode                    : Normal
Sequence Number                 : Single
Anti-Blur                       : On (Shooting)
Flashpix Version                : 0100
Color Space                     : sRGB
Exif Image Width                : 2592
Exif Image Height               : 1944
Interoperability Index          : R98 - DCF basic file (sRGB)
Interoperability Version        : 0100
File Source                     : Digital Camera
Scene Type                      : Directly photographed
Custom Rendered                 : Normal
Exposure Mode                   : Auto
White Balance                   : Auto
Scene Capture Type              : Standard
Contrast                        : Normal
Saturation                      : Normal
Sharpness                       : Normal
PrintIM Version                 : 0300
Compression                     : JPEG (old-style)
Thumbnail Offset                : 9384
Thumbnail Length                : 8953
Profile CMM Type                : appl
Profile Version                 : 2.2.0
Profile Class                   : Input Device Profile
Color Space Data                : RGB
Profile Connection Space        : XYZ
Profile Date Time               : 2003:07:01 00:00:00
Profile File Signature          : acsp
Primary Platform                : Apple Computer Inc.
CMM Flags                       : Not Embedded, Independent
Device Manufacturer             : appl
Device Model                    :
Device Attributes               : Reflective, Glossy, Positive, Color
Rendering Intent                : Perceptual
Connection Space Illuminant     : 0.9642 1 0.82491
Profile Creator                 : appl
Profile ID                      : 0
Red Matrix Column               : 0.45427 0.24263 0.01482
Green Matrix Column             : 0.35332 0.67441 0.09042
Blue Matrix Column              : 0.15662 0.08336 0.71953
Media White Point               : 0.95047 1 1.0891
Chromatic Adaptation            : 1.04788 0.02292 -0.0502 0.02957 0.99049 -0.01706 -0.00923 0.01508 0.75165
```

```
Red Tone Reproduction Curve    : (Binary data 14 bytes, use -b option to extract)
Green Tone Reproduction Curve  : (Binary data 14 bytes, use -b option to extract)
Blue Tone Reproduction Curve   : (Binary data 14 bytes, use -b option to extract)
Profile Description            : Camera RGB Profile
Profile Copyright              : Copyright 2003 Apple Computer Inc., all rights reserved.
Profile Description ML         : Camera RGB Profile
Profile Description ML (es-ES) : Perfil RGB para Cámara
Profile Description ML (da-DK) : RGB-beskrivelse til Kamera
Profile Description ML (de-DE) : RGB-Profil für Kameras
Profile Description ML (fi-FI) : Kameran RGB-profiili
Profile Description ML (fr-FU) : Profil RVB de l'appareil-photo
Profile Description ML (it-IT) : Profilo RGB Fotocamera
Profile Description ML (nl-NL) : RGB-profiel Camera
Profile Description ML (no-NO) : RGB-kameraprofil
Profile Description ML (pt-BR) : Perfil RGB de Câmera
Profile Description ML (sv-SE) : RGB-profil för Kamera
Profile Description ML (ja-JP) : カメラ RGB プロファイル
Profile Description ML (ko-KR) : 카메라 RGB 프로파일
Profile Description ML (zh-TW) : 數位相機 RGB 色彩描述
Profile Description ML (zh-CN) : 相机 RGB 描述文件
Image Width                    : 2592
Image Height                   : 1944
Encoding Process               : Baseline DCT, Huffman coding
Bits Per Sample                : 8
Color Components               : 3
Y Cb Cr Sub Sampling           : YCbCr4:2:2 (2 1)
Aperture                       : 5.0
Image Size                     : 2592x1944
Megapixels                     : 5.0
Shutter Speed                  : 1/13
Thumbnail Image                : (Binary data 8953 bytes, use -b option to extract)
Focal Length                   : 15.1 mm
Light Value                    : 6.3
```

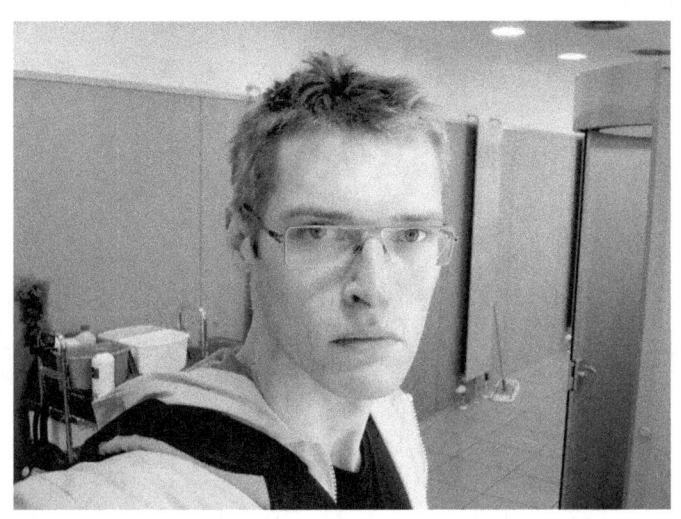

```
ExifTool Version Number         : 10.05
File Name                       : DSC01606.JPG
Directory                       : ../Selection
File Size                       : 1840 kB
File Modification Date/Time     : 2008:05:24 12:40:56+02:00
File Access Date/Time           : 2015:11:29 14:04:32+01:00
File Inode Change Date/Time     : 2015:11:05 21:35:08+01:00
File Permissions                : rw-r--r--
File Type                       : JPEG
File Type Extension             : jpg
MIME Type                       : image/jpeg
Exif Byte Order                 : Little-endian (Intel, II)
Image Description               :
Make                            : SONY
Camera Model Name               : DSC-W80
Orientation                     : Horizontal (normal)
X Resolution                    : 72
Y Resolution                    : 72
Resolution Unit                 : inches
Modify Date                     : 2008:05:22 21:14:00
Y Cb Cr Positioning             : Co-sited
Exposure Time                   : 1/20
F Number                        : 3.2
Exposure Program                : Program AE
ISO                             : 400
Exif Version                    : 0221
Date/Time Original              : 2008:05:22 21:14:00
Create Date                     : 2008:05:22 21:14:00
Components Configuration        : Y, Cb, Cr, -
Compressed Bits Per Pixel       : 4
Exposure Compensation           : 0
Max Aperture Value              : 2.8
Metering Mode                   : Multi-segment
Light Source                    : Unknown
Flash                           : Off, Did not fire
Focal Length                    : 6.6 mm
Creative Style                  : Standard
Macro                           : Off
Focus Mode                      : AF-S
AF Area Mode                    : Default
AF Illuminator                  : Off
JPEG Quality                    : Standard
Flash Level                     : Normal
Release Mode                    : Normal
Sequence Number                 : Single
Anti-Blur                       : On (Shooting)
Flashpix Version                : 0100
Color Space                     : sRGB
Exif Image Width                : 2592
Exif Image Height               : 1944
Interoperability Index          : R98 - DCF basic file (sRGB)
Interoperability Version        : 0100
File Source                     : Digital Camera
Scene Type                      : Directly photographed
Custom Rendered                 : Normal
Exposure Mode                   : Auto
White Balance                   : Auto
Scene Capture Type              : Standard
Contrast                        : Normal
Saturation                      : Normal
Sharpness                       : Normal
PrintIM Version                 : 0300
Compression                     : JPEG (old-style)
Thumbnail Offset                : 9384
Thumbnail Length                : 11143
Profile CMM Type                : appl
Profile Version                 : 2.2.0
Profile Class                   : Input Device Profile
Color Space Data                : RGB
Profile Connection Space        : XYZ
Profile Date Time               : 2003:07:01 00:00:00
Profile File Signature          : acsp
Primary Platform                : Apple Computer Inc.
CMM Flags                       : Not Embedded, Independent
Device Manufacturer             : appl
Device Model                    :
Device Attributes               : Reflective, Glossy, Positive, Color
Rendering Intent                : Perceptual
Connection Space Illuminant     : 0.9642 1 0.82491
Profile Creator                 : appl
Profile ID                      : 0
Red Matrix Column               : 0.45427 0.24263 0.01482
Green Matrix Column             : 0.35332 0.67441 0.09042
Blue Matrix Column              : 0.15662 0.08336 0.71953
Media White Point               : 0.95047 1 1.0891
Chromatic Adaptation            : 1.04788 0.02292 -0.0502 0.02957 0.99049 -0.01706 -0.00923 0.01508 0.75165
```

```
Red Tone Reproduction Curve      : (Binary data 14 bytes, use -b option to extract)
Green Tone Reproduction Curve    : (Binary data 14 bytes, use -b option to extract)
Blue Tone Reproduction Curve     : (Binary data 14 bytes, use -b option to extract)
Profile Description              : Camera RGB Profile
Profile Copyright                : Copyright 2003 Apple Computer Inc., all rights reserved.
Profile Description ML           : Camera RGB Profile
Profile Description ML (es-ES)   : Perfil RGB para Cámara
Profile Description ML (da-DK)   : RGB-beskrivelse til Kamera
Profile Description ML (de-DE)   : RGB-Profil für Kameras
Profile Description ML (fi-FI)   : Kameran RGB-profiili
Profile Description ML (fr-FU)   : Profil RVB de l'appareil-photo
Profile Description ML (it-IT)   : Profilo RGB Fotocamera
Profile Description ML (nl-NL)   : RGB-profiel Camera
Profile Description ML (no-NO)   : RGB-kameraprofil
Profile Description ML (pt-BR)   : Perfil RGB de Câmera
Profile Description ML (sv-SE)   : RGB-profil för Kamera
Profile Description ML (ja-JP)   : カメラ RGB プロファイル
Profile Description ML (ko-KR)   : 카메라 RGB 프로파일
Profile Description ML (zh-TW)   : 數位相機 RGB 色彩描述
Profile Description ML (zh-CN)   : 相机 RGB 描述文件
Image Width                      : 2592
Image Height                     : 1944
Encoding Process                 : Baseline DCT, Huffman coding
Bits Per Sample                  : 8
Color Components                 : 3
Y Cb Cr Sub Sampling             : YCbCr4:2:2 (2 1)
Aperture                         : 3.2
Image Size                       : 2592x1944
Megapixels                       : 5.0
Shutter Speed                    : 1/20
Thumbnail Image                  : (Binary data 11143 bytes, use -b option to extract)
Focal Length                     : 6.6 mm
Light Value                      : 5.7
```

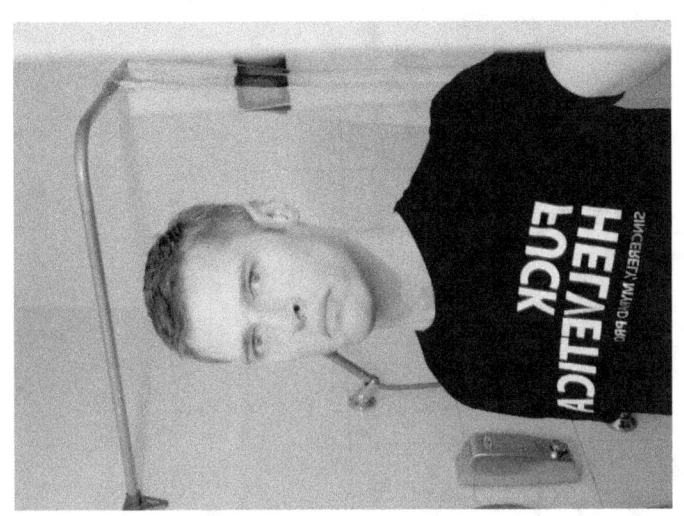

```
ExifTool Version Number         : 10.05
File Name                       : DSC01968.JPG
Directory                       : ../Selection
File Size                       : 1587 kB
File Modification Date/Time     : 2008:07:19 15:30:45+02:00
File Access Date/Time           : 2015:11:29 14:04:33+01:00
File Inode Change Date/Time     : 2015:11:05 21:35:08+01:00
File Permissions                : rw-r--r--
File Type                       : JPEG
File Type Extension             : jpg
MIME Type                       : image/jpeg
Exif Byte Order                 : Little-endian (Intel, II)
Image Description               :
Make                            : SONY
Camera Model Name               : DSC-W80
Orientation                     : Rotate 90 CW
X Resolution                    : 72
Y Resolution                    : 72
Resolution Unit                 : inches
Modify Date                     : 2008:07:16 18:28:39
Y Cb Cr Positioning             : Co-sited
Exposure Time                   : 1/10
F Number                        : 3.5
Exposure Program                : Program AE
ISO                             : 400
Exif Version                    : 0221
Date/Time Original              : 2008:07:16 18:28:39
Create Date                     : 2008:07:16 18:28:39
Components Configuration        : Y, Cb, Cr, -
Compressed Bits Per Pixel       : 4
Exposure Compensation           : 0
Max Aperture Value              : 2.8
Metering Mode                   : Multi-segment
Light Source                    : Unknown
Flash                           : Off, Did not fire
Focal Length                    : 8.7 mm
Creative Style                  : Standard
Macro                           : Off
Focus Mode                      : AF-S
AF Area Mode                    : Multi
AF Illuminator                  : Off
JPEG Quality                    : Standard
Flash Level                     : Normal
Release Mode                    : Normal
Sequence Number                 : Single
Anti-Blur                       : On (Shooting)
Flashpix Version                : 0100
Color Space                     : sRGB
Exif Image Width                : 2592
Exif Image Height               : 1944
Interoperability Index          : R98 - DCF basic file (sRGB)
Interoperability Version        : 0100
File Source                     : Digital Camera
Scene Type                      : Directly photographed
Custom Rendered                 : Normal
Exposure Mode                   : Auto
White Balance                   : Auto
Scene Capture Type              : Standard
Contrast                        : Normal
Saturation                      : Normal
Sharpness                       : Normal
PrintIM Version                 : 0300
Compression                     : JPEG (old-style)
Thumbnail Offset                : 9384
Thumbnail Length                : 9053
Profile CMM Type                : appl
Profile Version                 : 2.2.0
Profile Class                   : Input Device Profile
Color Space Data                : RGB
Profile Connection Space        : XYZ
Profile Date Time               : 2003:07:01 00:00:00
Profile File Signature          : acsp
Primary Platform                : Apple Computer Inc.
CMM Flags                       : Not Embedded, Independent
Device Manufacturer             : appl
Device Model                    :
Device Attributes               : Reflective, Glossy, Positive, Color
Rendering Intent                : Perceptual
Connection Space Illuminant     : 0.9642 1 0.82491
Profile Creator                 : appl
Profile ID                      : 0
Red Matrix Column               : 0.45427 0.24263 0.01482
Green Matrix Column             : 0.35332 0.67441 0.09042
Blue Matrix Column              : 0.15662 0.08336 0.71953
Media White Point               : 0.95047 1 1.0891
Chromatic Adaptation            : 1.04788 0.02292 -0.0502 0.02957 0.99049 -0.01706 -0.00923 0.01508 0.75165
```

```
Red Tone Reproduction Curve       : (Binary data 14 bytes, use -b option to extract)
Green Tone Reproduction Curve     : (Binary data 14 bytes, use -b option to extract)
Blue Tone Reproduction Curve      : (Binary data 14 bytes, use -b option to extract)
Profile Description               : Camera RGB Profile
Profile Copyright                 : Copyright 2003 Apple Computer Inc., all rights reserved.
Profile Description ML            : Camera RGB Profile
Profile Description ML (es-ES)    : Perfil RGB para Cámara
Profile Description ML (da-DK)    : RGB-beskrivelse til Kamera
Profile Description ML (de-DE)    : RGB-Profil für Kameras
Profile Description ML (fi-FI)    : Kameran RGB-profiili
Profile Description ML (fr-FU)    : Profil RVB de l'appareil-photo
Profile Description ML (it-IT)    : Profilo RGB Fotocamera
Profile Description ML (nl-NL)    : RGB-profiel Camera
Profile Description ML (no-NO)    : RGB-kameraprofil
Profile Description ML (pt-BR)    : Perfil RGB de Câmera
Profile Description ML (sv-SE)    : RGB-profil för Kamera
Profile Description ML (ja-JP)    : カメラ RGB プロファイル
Profile Description ML (ko-KR)    : 카메라 RGB 프로파일
Profile Description ML (zh-TW)    : 數位相機 RGB 色彩描述
Profile Description ML (zh-CN)    : 相机 RGB 描述文件
Image Width                       : 2592
Image Height                      : 1944
Encoding Process                  : Baseline DCT, Huffman coding
Bits Per Sample                   : 8
Color Components                  : 3
Y Cb Cr Sub Sampling              : YCbCr4:2:2 (2 1)
Aperture                          : 3.5
Image Size                        : 2592x1944
Megapixels                        : 5.0
Shutter Speed                     : 1/10
Thumbnail Image                   : (Binary data 9053 bytes, use -b option to extract)
Focal Length                      : 8.7 mm
Light Value                       : 4.9
```

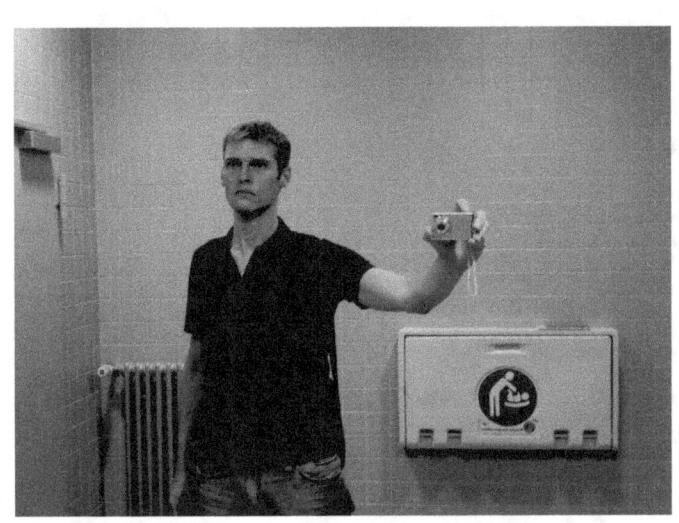

```
ExifTool Version Number         : 10.05
File Name                       : DSC02168.JPG
Directory                       : ../Selection
File Size                       : 1779 kB
File Modification Date/Time     : 2008:09:15 20:08:04+02:00
File Access Date/Time           : 2015:11:29 14:04:33+01:00
File Inode Change Date/Time     : 2015:11:05 21:35:08+01:00
File Permissions                : rw-r--r--
File Type                       : JPEG
File Type Extension             : jpg
MIME Type                       : image/jpeg
Exif Byte Order                 : Little-endian (Intel, II)
Image Description               :
Make                            : SONY
Camera Model Name               : DSC-W80
Orientation                     : Horizontal (normal)
X Resolution                    : 72
Y Resolution                    : 72
Resolution Unit                 : inches
Modify Date                     : 2008:09:09 14:35:56
Y Cb Cr Positioning             : Co-sited
Exposure Time                   : 1/20
F Number                        : 3.5
Exposure Program                : Program AE
ISO                             : 400
Exif Version                    : 0221
Date/Time Original              : 2008:09:09 14:35:56
Create Date                     : 2008:09:09 14:35:56
Components Configuration        : Y, Cb, Cr, -
Compressed Bits Per Pixel       : 4
Exposure Compensation           : -1
Max Aperture Value              : 2.8
Metering Mode                   : Multi-segment
Light Source                    : Unknown
Flash                           : Off, Did not fire
Focal Length                    : 8.7 mm
Creative Style                  : Standard
Macro                           : Off
Focus Mode                      : AF-S
AF Area Mode                    : Multi
AF Illuminator                  : Off
JPEG Quality                    : Standard
Flash Level                     : Normal
Release Mode                    : Normal
Sequence Number                 : Single
Anti-Blur                       : On (Shooting)
Flashpix Version                : 0100
Color Space                     : sRGB
Exif Image Width                : 2592
Exif Image Height               : 1944
Interoperability Index          : R98 - DCF basic file (sRGB)
Interoperability Version        : 0100
File Source                     : Digital Camera
Scene Type                      : Directly photographed
Custom Rendered                 : Normal
Exposure Mode                   : Manual
White Balance                   : Auto
Scene Capture Type              : Standard
Contrast                        : Normal
Saturation                      : Normal
Sharpness                       : Normal
PrintIM Version                 : 0300
Compression                     : JPEG (old-style)
Thumbnail Offset                : 9384
Thumbnail Length                : 7376
Profile CMM Type                : appl
Profile Version                 : 2.2.0
Profile Class                   : Input Device Profile
Color Space Data                : RGB
Profile Connection Space        : XYZ
Profile Date Time               : 2003:07:01 00:00:00
Profile File Signature          : acsp
Primary Platform                : Apple Computer Inc.
CMM Flags                       : Not Embedded, Independent
Device Manufacturer             : appl
Device Model                    :
Device Attributes               : Reflective, Glossy, Positive, Color
Rendering Intent                : Perceptual
Connection Space Illuminant     : 0.9642 1 0.82491
Profile Creator                 : appl
Profile ID                      : 0
Red Matrix Column               : 0.45427 0.24263 0.01482
Green Matrix Column             : 0.35332 0.67441 0.09042
Blue Matrix Column              : 0.15662 0.08336 0.71953
Media White Point               : 0.95047 1 1.0891
Chromatic Adaptation            : 1.04788 0.02292 -0.0502 0.02957 0.99049 -0.01706 -0.00923 0.01508 0.75165
```

```
Red Tone Reproduction Curve    : (Binary data 14 bytes, use -b option to extract)
Green Tone Reproduction Curve  : (Binary data 14 bytes, use -b option to extract)
Blue Tone Reproduction Curve   : (Binary data 14 bytes, use -b option to extract)
Profile Description            : Camera RGB Profile
Profile Copyright              : Copyright 2003 Apple Computer Inc., all rights reserved.
Profile Description ML         : Camera RGB Profile
Profile Description ML (es-ES) : Perfil RGB para Cámara
Profile Description ML (da-DK) : RGB-beskrivelse til Kamera
Profile Description ML (de-DE) : RGB-Profil für Kameras
Profile Description ML (fi-FI) : Kameran RGB-profiili
Profile Description ML (fr-FU) : Profil RVB de l'appareil-photo
Profile Description ML (it-IT) : Profilo RGB Fotocamera
Profile Description ML (nl-NL) : RGB-profiel Camera
Profile Description ML (no-NO) : RGB-kameraprofil
Profile Description ML (pt-BR) : Perfil RGB de Câmera
Profile Description ML (sv-SE) : RGB-profil för Kamera
Profile Description ML (ja-JP) : カメラ RGB プロファイル
Profile Description ML (ko-KR) : 카메라 RGB 프로파일
Profile Description ML (zh-TW) : 數位相機 RGB 色彩描述
Profile Description ML (zh-CN) : 相机 RGB 描述文件
Image Width                    : 2592
Image Height                   : 1944
Encoding Process               : Baseline DCT, Huffman coding
Bits Per Sample                : 8
Color Components               : 3
Y Cb Cr Sub Sampling           : YCbCr4:2:2 (2 1)
Aperture                       : 3.5
Image Size                     : 2592x1944
Megapixels                     : 5.0
Shutter Speed                  : 1/20
Thumbnail Image                : (Binary data 7376 bytes, use -b option to extract)
Focal Length                   : 8.7 mm
Light Value                    : 5.9
```

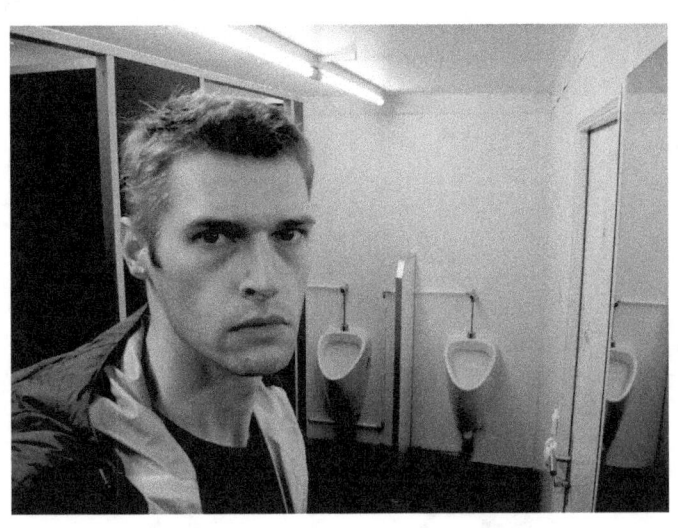

```
ExifTool Version Number        : 10.05
File Name                      : DSC02371.JPG
Directory                      : ../Selection
File Size                      : 1684 kB
File Modification Date/Time    : 2008:11:12 22:01:26+01:00
File Access Date/Time          : 2015:11:29 14:04:34+01:00
File Inode Change Date/Time    : 2015:11:05 21:35:08+01:00
File Permissions               : rw-r--r--
File Type                      : JPEG
File Type Extension            : jpg
MIME Type                      : image/jpeg
Exif Byte Order                : Little-endian (Intel, II)
Image Description              :
Make                           : SONY
Camera Model Name              : DSC-W80
Orientation                    : Horizontal (normal)
X Resolution                   : 72
Y Resolution                   : 72
Resolution Unit                : inches
Modify Date                    : 2008:10:25 21:42:17
Y Cb Cr Positioning            : Co-sited
Exposure Time                  : 1/60
F Number                       : 2.8
Exposure Program               : Program AE
ISO                            : 125
Exif Version                   : 0221
Date/Time Original             : 2008:10:25 21:42:17
Create Date                    : 2008:10:25 21:42:17
Components Configuration       : Y, Cb, Cr, -
Compressed Bits Per Pixel      : 4
Exposure Compensation          : -0.3
Max Aperture Value             : 2.8
Metering Mode                  : Multi-segment
Light Source                   : Unknown
Flash                          : Off, Did not fire
Focal Length                   : 5.8 mm
Creative Style                 : Standard
Macro                          : Off
Focus Mode                     : AF-S
AF Area Mode                   : Multi
AF Illuminator                 : Off
JPEG Quality                   : Standard
Flash Level                    : Normal
Release Mode                   : Normal
Sequence Number                : Single
Anti-Blur                      : On (Shooting)
Flashpix Version               : 0100
Color Space                    : sRGB
Exif Image Width               : 2592
Exif Image Height              : 1944
Interoperability Index         : R98 - DCF basic file (sRGB)
Interoperability Version       : 0100
File Source                    : Digital Camera
Scene Type                     : Directly photographed
Custom Rendered                : Normal
Exposure Mode                  : Manual
White Balance                  : Auto
Scene Capture Type             : Standard
Contrast                       : Normal
Saturation                     : Normal
Sharpness                      : Normal
PrintIM Version                : 0300
Compression                    : JPEG (old-style)
Thumbnail Offset               : 9384
Thumbnail Length               : 9658
Profile CMM Type               : appl
Profile Version                : 2.2.0
Profile Class                  : Input Device Profile
Color Space Data               : RGB
Profile Connection Space       : XYZ
Profile Date Time              : 2003:07:01 00:00:00
Profile File Signature         : acsp
Primary Platform               : Apple Computer Inc.
CMM Flags                      : Not Embedded, Independent
Device Manufacturer            : appl
Device Model                   :
Device Attributes              : Reflective, Glossy, Positive, Color
Rendering Intent               : Perceptual
Connection Space Illuminant    : 0.9642 1 0.82491
Profile Creator                : appl
Profile ID                     : 0
Red Matrix Column              : 0.45427 0.24263 0.01482
Green Matrix Column            : 0.35332 0.67441 0.09042
Blue Matrix Column             : 0.15662 0.08336 0.71953
Media White Point              : 0.95047 1 1.0891
Chromatic Adaptation           : 1.04788 0.02292 -0.0502 0.02957 0.99049 -0.01706 -0.00923 0.01508 0.75165
```

```
Red Tone Reproduction Curve     : (Binary data 14 bytes, use -b option to extract)
Green Tone Reproduction Curve   : (Binary data 14 bytes, use -b option to extract)
Blue Tone Reproduction Curve    : (Binary data 14 bytes, use -b option to extract)
Profile Description             : Camera RGB Profile
Profile Copyright               : Copyright 2003 Apple Computer Inc., all rights reserved.
Profile Description ML          : Camera RGB Profile
Profile Description ML (es-ES)  : Perfil RGB para Cámara
Profile Description ML (da-DK)  : RGB-beskrivelse til Kamera
Profile Description ML (de-DE)  : RGB-Profil für Kameras
Profile Description ML (fi-FI)  : Kameran RGB-profiili
Profile Description ML (fr-FU)  : Profil RVB de l'appareil-photo
Profile Description ML (it-IT)  : Profilo RGB Fotocamera
Profile Description ML (nl-NL)  : RGB-profiel Camera
Profile Description ML (no-NO)  : RGB-kameraprofil
Profile Description ML (pt-BR)  : Perfil RGB de Câmera
Profile Description ML (sv-SE)  : RGB-profil för Kamera
Profile Description ML (ja-JP)  : カメラ RGB プロファイル
Profile Description ML (ko-KR)  : 카메라 RGB 프로파일
Profile Description ML (zh-TW)  : 數位相機 RGB 色彩描述
Profile Description ML (zh-CN)  : 相机 RGB 描述文件
Image Width                     : 2592
Image Height                    : 1944
Encoding Process                : Baseline DCT, Huffman coding
Bits Per Sample                 : 8
Color Components                : 3
Y Cb Cr Sub Sampling            : YCbCr4:2:2 (2 1)
Aperture                        : 2.8
Image Size                      : 2592x1944
Megapixels                      : 5.0
Shutter Speed                   : 1/60
Thumbnail Image                 : (Binary data 9658 bytes, use -b option to extract)
Focal Length                    : 5.8 mm
Light Value                     : 8.6
```

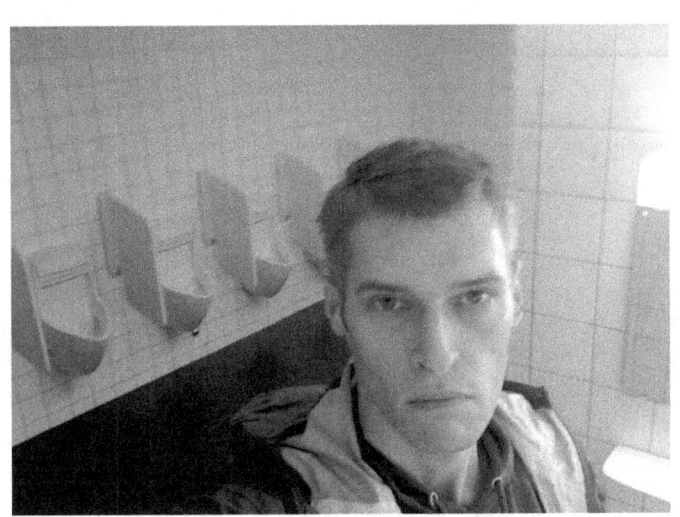

```
ExifTool Version Number        : 10.05
File Name                      : IMG_0049.JPG
Directory                      : ../Selection
File Size                      : 473 kB
File Modification Date/Time    : 2008:11:12 12:37:53+01:00
File Access Date/Time          : 2015:11:29 14:04:34+01:00
File Inode Change Date/Time    : 2015:11:05 21:35:08+01:00
File Permissions               : rw-r--r--
File Type                      : JPEG
File Type Extension            : jpg
MIME Type                      : image/jpeg
Exif Byte Order                : Big-endian (Motorola, MM)
Make                           : Apple
Camera Model Name              : iPhone
Orientation                    : Horizontal (normal)
X Resolution                   : 72
Y Resolution                   : 72
Resolution Unit                : inches
Software                       : QuickTime 7.5.5
Modify Date                    : 2008:11:12 12:37:53
Host Computer                  : Mac OS X 10.5.5
Y Cb Cr Positioning            : Centered
F Number                       : 2.8
Exif Version                   : 0220
Date/Time Original             : 2008:11:06 18:32:04
Create Date                    : 2008:11:06 18:32:04
Color Space                    : Uncalibrated
Exif Image Width               : 1600
Exif Image Height              : 1200
GPS Latitude Ref               : North
GPS Longitude Ref              : East
GPS Time Stamp                 : 18:31:25.38
Compression                    : JPEG (old-style)
Thumbnail Offset               : 646
Thumbnail Length               : 4310
Comment                        : AppleMark.
Image Width                    : 1600
Image Height                   : 1200
Encoding Process               : Baseline DCT, Huffman coding
Bits Per Sample                : 8
Color Components               : 3
Y Cb Cr Sub Sampling           : YCbCr4:2:2 (2 1)
Aperture                       : 2.8
GPS Latitude                   : 47 deg 24' 31.20" N
GPS Longitude                  : 8 deg 30' 19.80" E
GPS Position                   : 47 deg 24' 31.20" N, 8 deg 30' 19.80" E
Image Size                     : 1600x1200
Megapixels                     : 1.9
Thumbnail Image                : (Binary data 4310 bytes, use -b option to extract)
```

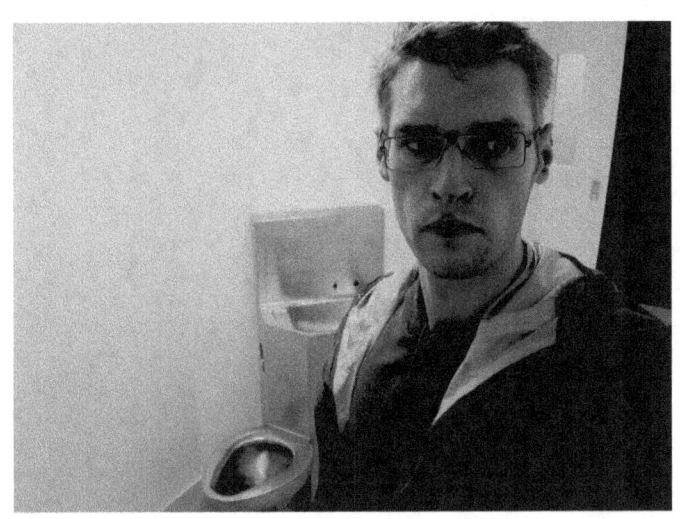

```
ExifTool Version Number         : 10.05
File Name                       : DSC02422.JPG
Directory                       : ../Selection
File Size                       : 1861 kB
File Modification Date/Time     : 2008:11:12 22:01:53+01:00
File Access Date/Time           : 2015:11:29 14:04:34+01:00
File Inode Change Date/Time     : 2015:11:05 21:35:08+01:00
File Permissions                : rw-r--r--
File Type                       : JPEG
File Type Extension             : jpg
MIME Type                       : image/jpeg
Exif Byte Order                 : Little-endian (Intel, II)
Image Description               :
Make                            : SONY
Camera Model Name               : DSC-W80
Orientation                     : Horizontal (normal)
X Resolution                    : 72
Y Resolution                    : 72
Resolution Unit                 : inches
Modify Date                     : 2008:11:08 16:02:26
Y Cb Cr Positioning             : Co-sited
Exposure Time                   : 1/40
F Number                        : 2.8
Exposure Program                : Program AE
ISO                             : 125
Exif Version                    : 0221
Date/Time Original              : 2008:11:08 16:02:26
Create Date                     : 2008:11:08 16:02:26
Components Configuration        : Y, Cb, Cr, -
Compressed Bits Per Pixel       : 4
Exposure Compensation           : -0.3
Max Aperture Value              : 2.8
Metering Mode                   : Multi-segment
Light Source                    : Unknown
Flash                           : Off, Did not fire
Focal Length                    : 5.8 mm
Creative Style                  : Standard
Macro                           : Off
Focus Mode                      : AF-S
AF Area Mode                    : Multi
AF Illuminator                  : Off
JPEG Quality                    : Standard
Flash Level                     : Normal
Release Mode                    : Normal
Sequence Number                 : Single
Anti-Blur                       : On (Shooting)
Flashpix Version                : 0100
Color Space                     : sRGB
Exif Image Width                : 2592
Exif Image Height               : 1944
Interoperability Index          : R98 - DCF basic file (sRGB)
Interoperability Version        : 0100
File Source                     : Digital Camera
Scene Type                      : Directly photographed
Custom Rendered                 : Normal
Exposure Mode                   : Manual
White Balance                   : Auto
Scene Capture Type              : Standard
Contrast                        : Normal
Saturation                      : Normal
Sharpness                       : Normal
PrintIM Version                 : 0300
Compression                     : JPEG (old-style)
Thumbnail Offset                : 9384
Thumbnail Length                : 7610
Profile CMM Type                : appl
Profile Version                 : 2.2.0
Profile Class                   : Input Device Profile
Color Space Data                : RGB
Profile Connection Space        : XYZ
Profile Date Time               : 2003:07:01 00:00:00
Profile File Signature          : acsp
Primary Platform                : Apple Computer Inc.
CMM Flags                       : Not Embedded, Independent
Device Manufacturer             : appl
Device Model                    :
Device Attributes               : Reflective, Glossy, Positive, Color
Rendering Intent                : Perceptual
Connection Space Illuminant     : 0.9642 1 0.82491
Profile Creator                 : appl
Profile ID                      : 0
Red Matrix Column               : 0.45427 0.24263 0.01482
Green Matrix Column             : 0.35332 0.67441 0.09042
Blue Matrix Column              : 0.15662 0.08336 0.71953
Media White Point               : 0.95047 1 1.0891
Chromatic Adaptation            : 1.04788 0.02292 -0.0502 0.02957 0.99049 -0.01706 -0.00923 0.01508 0.75165
```

```
Red Tone Reproduction Curve      : (Binary data 14 bytes, use -b option to extract)
Green Tone Reproduction Curve    : (Binary data 14 bytes, use -b option to extract)
Blue Tone Reproduction Curve     : (Binary data 14 bytes, use -b option to extract)
Profile Description              : Camera RGB Profile
Profile Copyright                : Copyright 2003 Apple Computer Inc., all rights reserved.
Profile Description ML           : Camera RGB Profile
Profile Description ML (es-ES)   : Perfil RGB para Cámara
Profile Description ML (da-DK)   : RGB-beskrivelse til Kamera
Profile Description ML (de-DE)   : RGB-Profil für Kameras
Profile Description ML (fi-FI)   : Kameran RGB-profiili
Profile Description ML (fr-FU)   : Profil RVB de l'appareil-photo
Profile Description ML (it-IT)   : Profilo RGB Fotocamera
Profile Description ML (nl-NL)   : RGB-profiel Camera
Profile Description ML (no-NO)   : RGB-kameraprofil
Profile Description ML (pt-BR)   : Perfil RGB de Câmera
Profile Description ML (sv-SE)   : RGB-profil för Kamera
Profile Description ML (ja-JP)   : カメラ RGB プロファイル
Profile Description ML (ko-KR)   : 카메라 RGB 프로파일
Profile Description ML (zh-TW)   : 數位相機 RGB 色彩描述
Profile Description ML (zh-CN)   : 相机 RGB 描述文件
Image Width                      : 2592
Image Height                     : 1944
Encoding Process                 : Baseline DCT, Huffman coding
Bits Per Sample                  : 8
Color Components                 : 3
Y Cb Cr Sub Sampling             : YCbCr4:2:2 (2 1)
Aperture                         : 2.8
Image Size                       : 2592x1944
Megapixels                       : 5.0
Shutter Speed                    : 1/40
Thumbnail Image                  : (Binary data 7610 bytes, use -b option to extract)
Focal Length                     : 5.8 mm
Light Value                      : 8.0
```

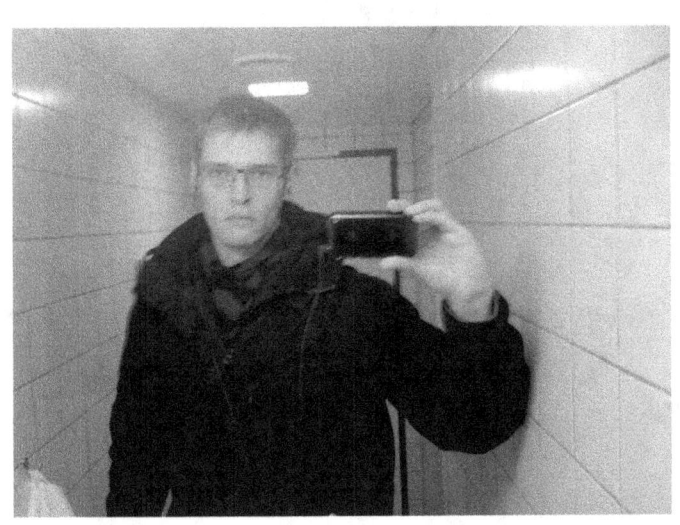

```
ExifTool Version Number         : 10.05
File Name                       : IMG_0076.JPG
Directory                       : ../Selection
File Size                       : 323 kB
Resource Fork Size              : 52 kB
File Modification Date/Time     : 2008:11:24 12:31:27+01:00
File Access Date/Time           : 2015:11:29 14:04:35+01:00
File Inode Change Date/Time     : 2015:11:05 21:35:08+01:00
File Permissions                : rw-r--r--
File Type                       : JPEG
File Type Extension             : jpg
MIME Type                       : image/jpeg
Exif Byte Order                 : Big-endian (Motorola, MM)
Make                            : Apple
Camera Model Name               : iPhone
Orientation                     : Horizontal (normal)
X Resolution                    : 72
Y Resolution                    : 72
Resolution Unit                 : inches
Modify Date                     : 2008:11:24 12:31:27
F Number                        : 2.8
Date/Time Original              : 2008:11:24 12:31:27
Create Date                     : 2008:11:24 12:31:27
Color Space                     : Uncalibrated
Exif Image Width                : 1600
Exif Image Height               : 1200
Gamma                           : 2.2
Compression                     : JPEG (old-style)
Thumbnail Offset                : 423
Thumbnail Length                : 6165
Image Width                     : 1600
Image Height                    : 1200
Encoding Process                : Baseline DCT, Huffman coding
Bits Per Sample                 : 8
Color Components                : 3
Y Cb Cr Sub Sampling            : YCbCr4:2:2 (2 1)
Aperture                        : 2.8
Image Size                      : 1600x1200
Megapixels                      : 1.9
Thumbnail Image                 : (Binary data 6165 bytes, use -b option to extract)
```

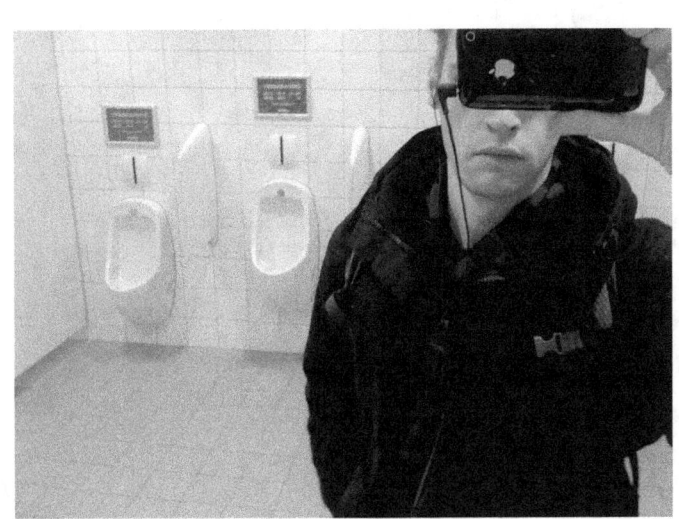

```
ExifTool Version Number        : 10.05
File Name                      : IMG_0089.JPG
Directory                      : ../Selection
File Size                      : 372 kB
Resource Fork Size             : 52 kB
File Modification Date/Time    : 2008:11:28 10:05:12+01:00
File Access Date/Time          : 2015:11:29 14:04:35+01:00
File Inode Change Date/Time    : 2015:11:29 12:37:00+01:00
File Permissions               : rw-r--r--
File Type                      : JPEG
File Type Extension            : jpg
MIME Type                      : image/jpeg
Exif Byte Order                : Big-endian (Motorola, MM)
Make                           : Apple
Camera Model Name              : iPhone
Orientation                    : Horizontal (normal)
X Resolution                   : 72
Y Resolution                   : 72
Resolution Unit                : inches
Modify Date                    : 2008:11:28 10:05:12
F Number                       : 2.8
Date/Time Original             : 2008:11:28 10:05:12
Create Date                    : 2008:11:28 10:05:12
Color Space                    : Uncalibrated
Exif Image Width               : 1600
Exif Image Height              : 1200
Gamma                          : 2.2
GPS Latitude Ref               : North
GPS Longitude Ref              : East
GPS Time Stamp                 : 10:04:57.26
Compression                    : JPEG (old-style)
Thumbnail Offset               : 573
Thumbnail Length               : 7211
Image Width                    : 1600
Image Height                   : 1200
Encoding Process               : Baseline DCT, Huffman coding
Bits Per Sample                : 8
Color Components               : 3
Y Cb Cr Sub Sampling           : YCbCr4:2:2 (2 1)
Aperture                       : 2.8
GPS Latitude                   : 47 deg 25' 3.00" N
GPS Longitude                  : 8 deg 24' 28.20" E
GPS Position                   : 47 deg 25' 3.00" N, 8 deg 24' 28.20" E
Image Size                     : 1600x1200
Megapixels                     : 1.9
Thumbnail Image                : (Binary data 7211 bytes, use -b option to extract)
```

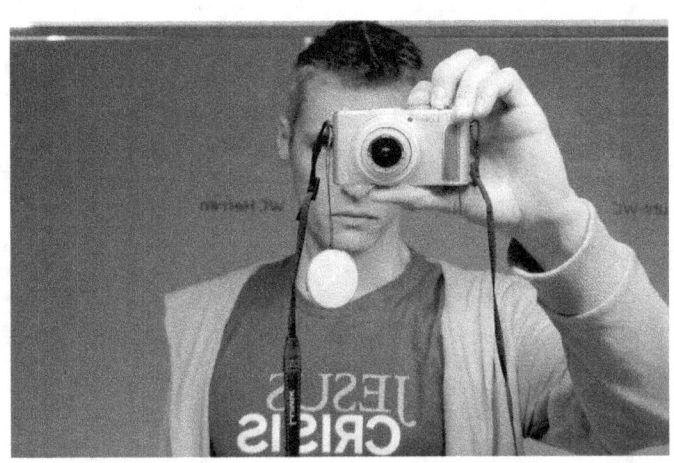

```
ExifTool Version Number         : 10.05
File Name                       : P1000071.JPG
Directory                       : ../Selection
File Size                       : 3.3 MB
File Modification Date/Time     : 2009:05:29 07:47:18+02:00
File Access Date/Time           : 2015:11:29 14:04:36+01:00
File Inode Change Date/Time     : 2015:11:05 21:35:08+01:00
File Permissions                : rw-r--r--
File Type                       : JPEG
File Type Extension             : jpg
MIME Type                       : image/jpeg
Exif Byte Order                 : Little-endian (Intel, II)
Make                            : Panasonic
Camera Model Name               : DMC-LX3
Orientation                     : Horizontal (normal)
X Resolution                    : 180
Y Resolution                    : 180
Resolution Unit                 : inches
Software                        : Ver.1.0
Modify Date                     : 2009:05:28 19:22:50
Y Cb Cr Positioning             : Co-sited
Exposure Time                   : 1/50
F Number                        : 2.8
Exposure Program                : Program AE
ISO                             : 400
Exif Version                    : 0221
Date/Time Original              : 2009:05:28 19:22:50
Create Date                     : 2009:05:28 19:22:50
Components Configuration        : Y, Cb, Cr, -
Compressed Bits Per Pixel       : 4
Exposure Compensation           : 0
Max Aperture Value              : 2.0
Metering Mode                   : Multi-segment
Light Source                    : Unknown
Flash                           : Off, Did not fire
Focal Length                    : 12.8 mm
Image Quality                   : High
Firmware Version                : 0.1.0.0
White Balance                   : Auto
Focus Mode                      : Auto
AF Area Mode                    : Tracking
Image Stabilization             : On, Mode 1
Macro Mode                      : Off
Shooting Mode                   : Intelligent Auto
Audio                           : No
Data Dump                       : (Binary data 8200 bytes, use -b option to extract)
Flash Bias                      : 0
Internal Serial Number          : (F37) 2008:09:24 no. 0023
Panasonic Exif Version          : 0270
Color Effect                    : Off
Time Since Power On             : 00:00:30.78
Burst Mode                      : Off
Sequence Number                 : 0
Contrast Mode                   : Normal
Noise Reduction                 : Standard
Self Timer                      : Off
Rotation                        : Horizontal (normal)
AF Assist Lamp                  : Enabled but Not Used
Color Mode                      : Normal
Optical Zoom Mode               : Standard
Conversion Lens                 : Off
Travel Day                      : n/a
World Time Location             : Home
Program ISO                     : n/a
Advanced Scene Type             : 5
Faces Detected                  : 0
Film Mode                       : n/a
Color Temp Kelvin               : 0
WB Shift AB                     : 0
WB Shift GM                     : 0
Flash Curtain                   : n/a
Panasonic Image Width           : 0
Panasonic Image Height          : 0
AF Point Position               : 0.5 0.5
Num Face Positions              : 0
Maker Note Version              : 0130
Scene Mode                      : Intelligent Auto
WB Red Level                    : 2011
WB Green Level                  : 1054
WB Blue Level                   : 2435
Flash Fired                     : No
Text Stamp                      : Off
Baby Age                        : (not set)
Flashpix Version                : 0100
Color Space                     : sRGB
Exif Image Width                : 3776
```

```
Exif Image Height              : 2520
Interoperability Index         : R98 - DCF basic file (sRGB)
Interoperability Version       : 0100
Sensing Method                 : One-chip color area
File Source                    : Digital Camera
Scene Type                     : Directly photographed
Custom Rendered                : Normal
Exposure Mode                  : Auto
Digital Zoom Ratio             : 0
Focal Length In 35mm Format    : 60 mm
Scene Capture Type             : Standard
Gain Control                   : High gain up
Contrast                       : Normal
Saturation                     : Normal
Sharpness                      : Normal
PrintIM Version                : 0250
Compression                    : JPEG (old-style)
Thumbnail Offset               : 10752
Thumbnail Length               : 5404
Profile CMM Type               : appl
Profile Version                : 2.2.0
Profile Class                  : Input Device Profile
Color Space Data               : RGB
Profile Connection Space       : XYZ
Profile Date Time              : 2003:07:01 00:00:00
Profile File Signature         : acsp
Primary Platform               : Apple Computer Inc.
CMM Flags                      : Not Embedded, Independent
Device Manufacturer            : appl
Device Model                   :
Device Attributes              : Reflective, Glossy, Positive, Color
Rendering Intent               : Perceptual
Connection Space Illuminant    : 0.9642 1 0.82491
Profile Creator                : appl
Profile ID                     : 0
Red Matrix Column              : 0.45427 0.24263 0.01482
Green Matrix Column            : 0.35332 0.67441 0.09042
Blue Matrix Column             : 0.15662 0.08336 0.71953
Media White Point              : 0.95047 1 1.0891
Chromatic Adaptation           : 1.04788 0.02292 -0.0502 0.02957 0.99049 -0.01706 -0.00923 0.01508 0.75165
Red Tone Reproduction Curve    : (Binary data 14 bytes, use -b option to extract)
Green Tone Reproduction Curve  : (Binary data 14 bytes, use -b option to extract)
Blue Tone Reproduction Curve   : (Binary data 14 bytes, use -b option to extract)
Profile Description            : Camera RGB Profile
Profile Copyright              : Copyright 2003 Apple Computer Inc., all rights reserved.
Profile Description ML         : Camera RGB Profile
Profile Description ML (es-ES) : Perfil RGB para Cámara
Profile Description ML (da-DK) : RGB-beskrivelse til Kamera
Profile Description ML (de-DE) : RGB-Profil für Kameras
Profile Description ML (fi-FI) : Kameran RGB-profiili
Profile Description ML (fr-FU) : Profil RVB de l'appareil-photo
Profile Description ML (it-IT) : Profilo RGB Fotocamera
Profile Description ML (nl-NL) : RGB-profiel Camera
Profile Description ML (no-NO) : RGB-kameraprofil
Profile Description ML (pt-BR) : Perfil RGB de Câmera
Profile Description ML (sv-SE) : RGB-profil för Kamera
Profile Description ML (ja-JP) : カメラ RGB プロファイル
Profile Description ML (ko-KR) : 카메라 RGB 프로파일
Profile Description ML (zh-TW) : 數位相機 RGB 色彩描述
Profile Description ML (zh-CN) : 相机 RGB 描述文件
Image Width                    : 3776
Image Height                   : 2520
Encoding Process               : Baseline DCT, Huffman coding
Bits Per Sample                : 8
Color Components               : 3
Y Cb Cr Sub Sampling           : YCbCr4:2:2 (2 1)
Advanced Scene Mode            : Intelligent Auto (intelligent auto)
Aperture                       : 2.8
Blue Balance                   : 2.310247
Image Size                     : 3776x2520
Megapixels                     : 9.5
Red Balance                    : 1.90797
Scale Factor To 35 mm Equivalent: 4.7
Shutter Speed                  : 1/50
Thumbnail Image                : (Binary data 5404 bytes, use -b option to extract)
Circle Of Confusion            : 0.006 mm
Field Of View                  : 33.4 deg
Focal Length                   : 12.8 mm (35 mm equivalent: 60.0 mm)
Hyperfocal Distance            : 9.13 m
Light Value                    : 6.6
```

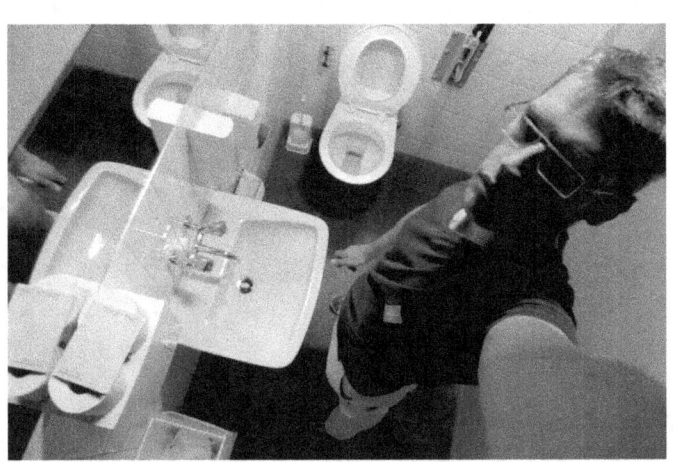

```
ExifTool Version Number         : 10.05
File Name                       : P1000202.JPG
Directory                       : ../Selection
File Size                       : 3.2 MB
File Modification Date/Time     : 2009:06:16 12:56:44+02:00
File Access Date/Time           : 2015:11:29 14:04:36+01:00
File Inode Change Date/Time     : 2015:11:05 21:35:08+01:00
File Permissions                : rwxr-xr-x
File Type                       : JPEG
File Type Extension             : jpg
MIME Type                       : image/jpeg
Exif Byte Order                 : Little-endian (Intel, II)
Make                            : Panasonic
Camera Model Name               : DMC-LX3
Orientation                     : Horizontal (normal)
X Resolution                    : 180
Y Resolution                    : 180
Resolution Unit                 : inches
Software                        : Ver.1.0
Modify Date                     : 2009:06:16 12:56:44
Y Cb Cr Positioning             : Co-sited
Exposure Time                   : 1/30
F Number                        : 2.0
Exposure Program                : Program AE
ISO                             : 320
Exif Version                    : 0221
Date/Time Original              : 2009:06:16 12:56:44
Create Date                     : 2009:06:16 12:56:44
Components Configuration        : Y, Cb, Cr, -
Compressed Bits Per Pixel       : 2
Exposure Compensation           : 0
Max Aperture Value              : 2.0
Metering Mode                   : Multi-segment
Light Source                    : Unknown
Flash                           : Off, Did not fire
Focal Length                    : 5.1 mm
Image Quality                   : Raw
Firmware Version                : 0.1.0.0
White Balance                   : Auto
Focus Mode                      : Auto
AF Area Mode                    : 1-area (high speed)
Image Stabilization             : On, Mode 2
Macro Mode                      : Off
Shooting Mode                   : Program
Audio                           : No
Data Dump                       : (Binary data 8200 bytes, use -b option to extract)
Flash Bias                      : 0
Internal Serial Number          : (F37) 2008:09:24 no. 0023
Panasonic Exif Version          : 0270
Color Effect                    : Off
Time Since Power On             : 00:00:55.71
Burst Mode                      : Off
Sequence Number                 : 0
Contrast Mode                   : Normal
Noise Reduction                 : Standard
Self Timer                      : Off
Rotation                        : Horizontal (normal)
AF Assist Lamp                  : Enabled but Not Used
Color Mode                      : Normal
Optical Zoom Mode               : Standard
Conversion Lens                 : Off
Travel Day                      : n/a
World Time Location             : Home
Program ISO                     : n/a
Advanced Scene Type             : 1
Faces Detected                  : 0
Film Mode                       : Standard (color)
Color Temp Kelvin               : 0
WB Shift AB                     : 0
WB Shift GM                     : 0
Flash Curtain                   : n/a
Panasonic Image Width           : 3776
Panasonic Image Height          : 2520
AF Point Position               : 0.5 0.5
Num Face Positions              : 0
Maker Note Version              : 0130
Scene Mode                      : Off
WB Red Level                    : 2285
WB Green Level                  : 1054
WB Blue Level                   : 1831
Flash Fired                     : No
Text Stamp                      : Off
Baby Age                        : (not set)
Flashpix Version                : 0100
Color Space                     : sRGB
Exif Image Width                : 3776
```

```
Exif Image Height              : 2520
Interoperability Index         : R98 - DCF basic file (sRGB)
Interoperability Version       : 0100
Sensing Method                 : One-chip color area
File Source                    : Digital Camera
Scene Type                     : Directly photographed
Custom Rendered                : Normal
Exposure Mode                  : Auto
Digital Zoom Ratio             : 0
Focal Length In 35mm Format    : 24 mm
Scene Capture Type             : Standard
Gain Control                   : High gain up
Contrast                       : Normal
Saturation                     : Normal
Sharpness                      : Normal
PrintIM Version                : 0250
Compression                    : JPEG (old-style)
Thumbnail Offset               : 10752
Thumbnail Length               : 6147
Image Width                    : 3776
Image Height                   : 2520
Encoding Process               : Baseline DCT, Huffman coding
Bits Per Sample                : 8
Color Components               : 3
Y Cb Cr Sub Sampling           : YCbCr4:2:2 (2 1)
Advanced Scene Mode            : Off
Aperture                       : 2.0
Blue Balance                   : 1.737192
Image Size                     : 3776x2520
Megapixels                     : 9.5
Red Balance                    : 2.167932
Scale Factor To 35 mm Equivalent: 4.7
Shutter Speed                  : 1/30
Thumbnail Image                : (Binary data 6147 bytes, use -b option to extract)
Circle Of Confusion            : 0.006 mm
Field Of View                  : 73.7 deg
Focal Length                   : 5.1 mm (35 mm equivalent: 24.0 mm)
Hyperfocal Distance            : 2.04 m
Light Value                    : 5.2
```

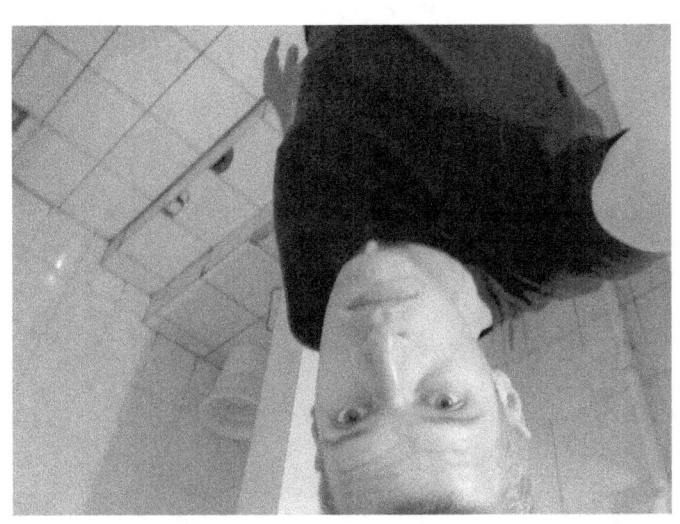

```
ExifTool Version Number         : 10.05
File Name                       : IMG_0258.JPG
Directory                       : ../Selection
File Size                       : 390 kB
Resource Fork Size              : 52 kB
File Modification Date/Time     : 2009:06:25 12:08:46+02:00
File Access Date/Time           : 2015:11:29 14:04:36+01:00
File Inode Change Date/Time     : 2015:11:05 21:35:08+01:00
File Permissions                : rw-r--r--
File Type                       : JPEG
File Type Extension             : jpg
MIME Type                       : image/jpeg
Exif Byte Order                 : Big-endian (Motorola, MM)
Make                            : Apple
Camera Model Name               : iPhone
Orientation                     : Rotate 180
X Resolution                    : 72
Y Resolution                    : 72
Resolution Unit                 : inches
Modify Date                     : 2009:06:25 12:08:46
F Number                        : 2.8
Date/Time Original              : 2009:06:25 12:08:46
Create Date                     : 2009:06:25 12:08:46
Color Space                     : sRGB
Exif Image Width                : 1600
Exif Image Height               : 1200
Gamma                           : 2.2
Compression                     : JPEG (old-style)
Thumbnail Offset                : 423
Thumbnail Length                : 6902
Image Width                     : 1600
Image Height                    : 1200
Encoding Process                : Baseline DCT, Huffman coding
Bits Per Sample                 : 8
Color Components                : 3
Y Cb Cr Sub Sampling            : YCbCr4:2:2 (2 1)
Aperture                        : 2.8
Image Size                      : 1600x1200
Megapixels                      : 1.9
Thumbnail Image                 : (Binary data 6902 bytes, use -b option to extract)
```

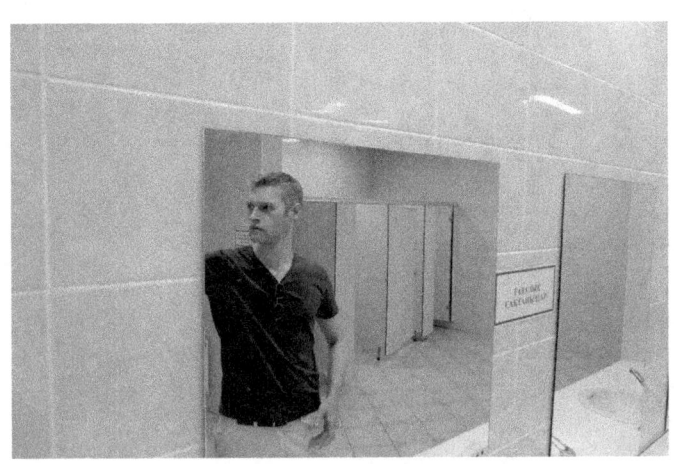

```
ExifTool Version Number        : 10.05
File Name                      : P1000438.JPG
Directory                      : ../Selection
File Size                      : 3.2 MB
Resource Fork Size             : 50 kB
File Modification Date/Time    : 2009:06:27 10:30:51+02:00
File Access Date/Time          : 2015:11:29 14:04:37+01:00
File Inode Change Date/Time    : 2015:11:05 21:35:08+01:00
File Permissions               : rw-r--r--
File Type                      : JPEG
File Type Extension            : jpg
MIME Type                      : image/jpeg
Exif Byte Order                : Little-endian (Intel, II)
Make                           : Panasonic
Camera Model Name              : DMC-LX3
Orientation                    : Horizontal (normal)
X Resolution                   : 180
Y Resolution                   : 180
Resolution Unit                : inches
Software                       : Ver.1.0
Modify Date                    : 2009:06:27 10:30:51
Y Cb Cr Positioning            : Co-sited
Exposure Time                  : 1/30
F Number                       : 2.0
Exposure Program               : Program AE
ISO                            : 400
Exif Version                   : 0221
Date/Time Original             : 2009:06:27 10:30:51
Create Date                    : 2009:06:27 10:30:51
Components Configuration       : Y, Cb, Cr, -
Compressed Bits Per Pixel      : 2
Exposure Compensation          : 0
Max Aperture Value             : 2.0
Metering Mode                  : Multi-segment
Light Source                   : Unknown
Flash                          : Off, Did not fire
Focal Length                   : 5.1 mm
Image Quality                  : Raw
Firmware Version               : 0.1.0.0
White Balance                  : Auto
Focus Mode                     : Auto
AF Area Mode                   : 1-area
Image Stabilization            : On, Mode 2
Macro Mode                     : Off
Shooting Mode                  : Program
Audio                          : No
Data Dump                      : (Binary data 8200 bytes, use -b option to extract)
Flash Bias                     : 0
Internal Serial Number         : (F37) 2008:09:24 no. 0023
Panasonic Exif Version         : 0270
Color Effect                   : Off
Time Since Power On            : 00:00:08.81
Burst Mode                     : Off
Sequence Number                : 0
Contrast Mode                  : Normal
Noise Reduction                : Standard
Self Timer                     : Off
Rotation                       : Horizontal (normal)
AF Assist Lamp                 : Enabled but Not Used
Color Mode                     : Normal
Optical Zoom Mode              : Standard
Conversion Lens                : Off
Travel Day                     : n/a
World Time Location            : Home
Program ISO                    : n/a
Advanced Scene Type            : 1
Faces Detected                 : 0
Film Mode                      : Standard (color)
Color Temp Kelvin              : 0
WB Shift AB                    : 0
WB Shift GM                    : 0
Flash Curtain                  : n/a
Panasonic Image Width          : 3776
Panasonic Image Height         : 2520
AF Point Position              : 0.5 0.5
Num Face Positions             : 0
Maker Note Version             : 0130
Scene Mode                     : Off
WB Red Level                   : 2011
WB Green Level                 : 1054
WB Blue Level                  : 2618
Flash Fired                    : No
Text Stamp                     : Off
Baby Age                       : (not set)
Flashpix Version               : 0100
Color Space                    : sRGB
```

```
Exif Image Width              : 3776
Exif Image Height             : 2520
Interoperability Index        : R98 - DCF basic file (sRGB)
Interoperability Version      : 0100
Sensing Method                : One-chip color area
File Source                   : Digital Camera
Scene Type                    : Directly photographed
Custom Rendered               : Normal
Exposure Mode                 : Auto
Digital Zoom Ratio            : 0
Focal Length In 35mm Format   : 24 mm
Scene Capture Type            : Standard
Gain Control                  : High gain up
Contrast                      : Normal
Saturation                    : Normal
Sharpness                     : Normal
PrintIM Version               : 0250
Compression                   : JPEG (old-style)
Thumbnail Offset              : 10752
Thumbnail Length              : 4468
Image Width                   : 3776
Image Height                  : 2520
Encoding Process              : Baseline DCT, Huffman coding
Bits Per Sample               : 8
Color Components              : 3
Y Cb Cr Sub Sampling          : YCbCr4:2:2 (2 1)
Advanced Scene Mode           : Off
Aperture                      : 2.0
Blue Balance                  : 2.483871
Image Size                    : 3776x2520
Megapixels                    : 9.5
Red Balance                   : 1.90797
Scale Factor To 35 mm Equivalent: 4.7
Shutter Speed                 : 1/30
Thumbnail Image               : (Binary data 4468 bytes, use -b option to extract)
Circle Of Confusion           : 0.006 mm
Field Of View                 : 73.7 deg
Focal Length                  : 5.1 mm (35 mm equivalent: 24.0 mm)
Hyperfocal Distance           : 2.04 m
Light Value                   : 4.9
```

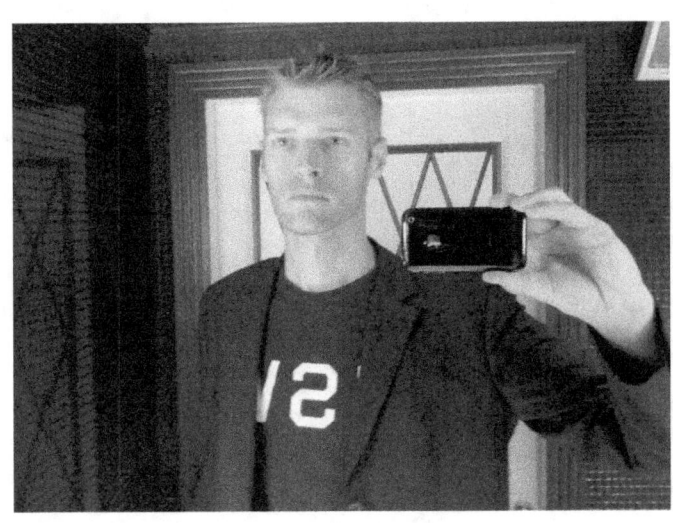

```
ExifTool Version Number         : 10.05
File Name                       : IMG_0262.JPG
Directory                       : ../Selection
File Size                       : 458 kB
Resource Fork Size              : 52 kB
File Modification Date/Time     : 2009:06:27 22:21:48+02:00
File Access Date/Time           : 2015:11:29 14:04:37+01:00
File Inode Change Date/Time     : 2015:11:05 21:35:08+01:00
File Permissions                : rw-r--r--
File Type                       : JPEG
File Type Extension             : jpg
MIME Type                       : image/jpeg
Exif Byte Order                 : Big-endian (Motorola, MM)
Make                            : Apple
Camera Model Name               : iPhone
Orientation                     : Horizontal (normal)
X Resolution                    : 72
Y Resolution                    : 72
Resolution Unit                 : inches
Modify Date                     : 2009:06:27 22:21:48
F Number                        : 2.8
Date/Time Original              : 2009:06:27 22:21:48
Create Date                     : 2009:06:27 22:21:48
Color Space                     : sRGB
Exif Image Width                : 1600
Exif Image Height               : 1200
Gamma                           : 2.2
Compression                     : JPEG (old-style)
Thumbnail Offset                : 423
Thumbnail Length                : 7600
Image Width                     : 1600
Image Height                    : 1200
Encoding Process                : Baseline DCT, Huffman coding
Bits Per Sample                 : 8
Color Components                : 3
Y Cb Cr Sub Sampling            : YCbCr4:2:2 (2 1)
Aperture                        : 2.8
Image Size                      : 1600x1200
Megapixels                      : 1.9
Thumbnail Image                 : (Binary data 7600 bytes, use -b option to extract)
```

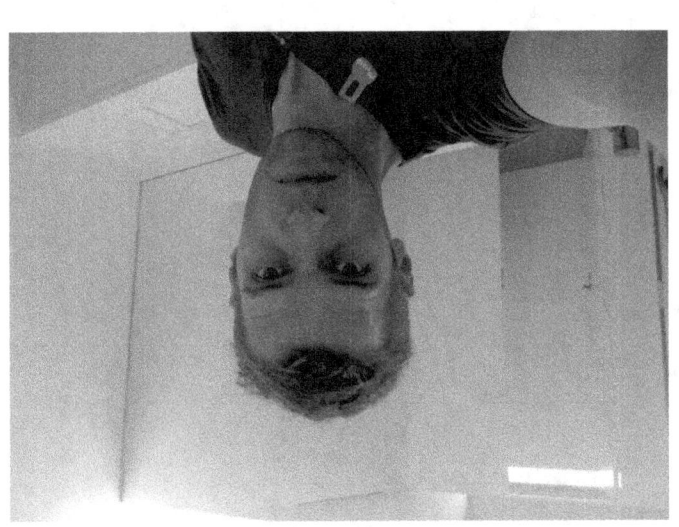

```
ExifTool Version Number        : 10.05
File Name                      : IMG_0271.JPG
Directory                      : ../Selection
File Size                      : 430 kB
Resource Fork Size             : 51 kB
File Modification Date/Time    : 2009:07:04 15:41:10+02:00
File Access Date/Time          : 2015:11:29 14:04:37+01:00
File Inode Change Date/Time    : 2015:11:05 21:35:08+01:00
File Permissions               : rw-r--r--
File Type                      : JPEG
File Type Extension            : jpg
MIME Type                      : image/jpeg
Exif Byte Order                : Big-endian (Motorola, MM)
Make                           : Apple
Camera Model Name              : iPhone
Orientation                    : Rotate 180
X Resolution                   : 72
Y Resolution                   : 72
Resolution Unit                : inches
Modify Date                    : 2009:07:04 15:41:10
Y Cb Cr Positioning            : Centered
F Number                       : 2.8
Exif Version                   : 0221
Date/Time Original             : 2009:07:04 15:41:10
Create Date                    : 2009:07:04 15:41:10
Components Configuration       : Y, Cb, Cr, -
Flashpix Version               : 0100
Color Space                    : sRGB
Exif Image Width               : 1600
Exif Image Height              : 1200
Compression                    : JPEG (old-style)
Thumbnail Offset               : 452
Thumbnail Length               : 5491
Image Width                    : 1600
Image Height                   : 1200
Encoding Process               : Baseline DCT, Huffman coding
Bits Per Sample                : 8
Color Components               : 3
Y Cb Cr Sub Sampling           : YCbCr4:2:0 (2 2)
Aperture                       : 2.8
Image Size                     : 1600x1200
Megapixels                     : 1.9
Thumbnail Image                : (Binary data 5491 bytes, use -b option to extract)
```

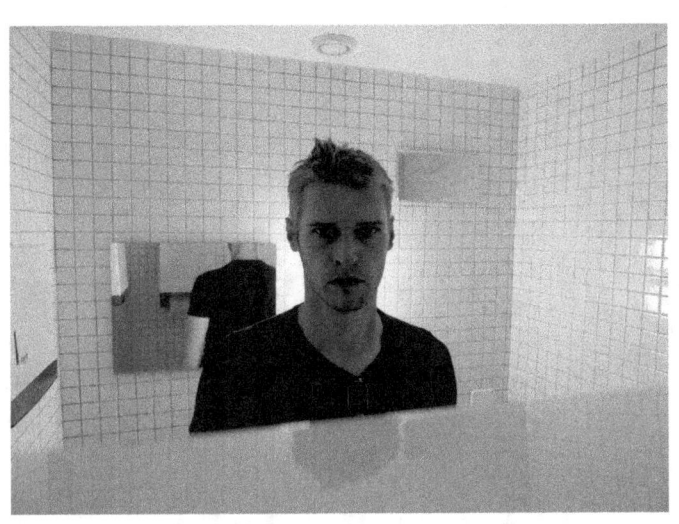

```
ExifTool Version Number         : 10.05
File Name                       : P1000526.JPG
Directory                       : ../Selection
File Size                       : 3.4 MB
Resource Fork Size              : 52 kB
File Modification Date/Time     : 2009:07:05 14:59:03+02:00
File Access Date/Time           : 2015:11:29 14:04:37+01:00
File Inode Change Date/Time     : 2015:11:05 21:35:08+01:00
File Permissions                : rw-r--r--
File Type                       : JPEG
File Type Extension             : jpg
MIME Type                       : image/jpeg
Exif Byte Order                 : Little-endian (Intel, II)
Make                            : Panasonic
Camera Model Name               : DMC-LX3
Orientation                     : Horizontal (normal)
X Resolution                    : 180
Y Resolution                    : 180
Resolution Unit                 : inches
Software                        : Ver.1.0
Modify Date                     : 2009:07:05 14:59:03
Y Cb Cr Positioning             : Co-sited
Exposure Time                   : 1/30
F Number                        : 2.0
Exposure Program                : Program AE
ISO                             : 320
Exif Version                    : 0221
Date/Time Original              : 2009:07:05 14:59:03
Create Date                     : 2009:07:05 14:59:03
Components Configuration        : Y, Cb, Cr, -
Compressed Bits Per Pixel       : 4
Exposure Compensation           : 0
Max Aperture Value              : 2.0
Metering Mode                   : Multi-segment
Light Source                    : Unknown
Flash                           : Off, Did not fire
Focal Length                    : 5.1 mm
Image Quality                   : High
Firmware Version                : 0.1.0.0
White Balance                   : Auto
Focus Mode                      : Manual
AF Area Mode                    : 1-area
Image Stabilization             : On, Mode 2
Macro Mode                      : Off
Shooting Mode                   : Program
Audio                           : No
Data Dump                       : (Binary data 8200 bytes, use -b option to extract)
Flash Bias                      : 0
Internal Serial Number          : (F37) 2008:09:24 no. 0023
Panasonic Exif Version          : 0270
Color Effect                    : Off
Time Since Power On             : 00:01:20.62
Burst Mode                      : Off
Sequence Number                 : 0
Contrast Mode                   : Normal
Noise Reduction                 : Standard
Self Timer                      : 2 s
Rotation                        : Horizontal (normal)
AF Assist Lamp                  : Enabled but Not Used
Color Mode                      : Normal
Optical Zoom Mode               : Standard
Conversion Lens                 : Off
Travel Day                      : n/a
World Time Location             : Home
Program ISO                     : n/a
Advanced Scene Type             : 1
Faces Detected                  : 0
Film Mode                       : Standard (color)
Color Temp Kelvin               : 0
WB Shift AB                     : 0
WB Shift GM                     : 0
Flash Curtain                   : n/a
Panasonic Image Width           : 0
Panasonic Image Height          : 0
AF Point Position               : none
Num Face Positions              : 0
Maker Note Version              : 0130
Scene Mode                      : Off
WB Red Level                    : 1279
WB Green Level                  : 1054
WB Blue Level                   : 2719
Flash Fired                     : No
Text Stamp                      : Off
Baby Age                        : (not set)
Flashpix Version                : 0100
Color Space                     : sRGB
```

```
Exif Image Width              : 3648
Exif Image Height             : 2736
Interoperability Index        : R98 - DCF basic file (sRGB)
Interoperability Version      : 0100
Sensing Method                : One-chip color area
File Source                   : Digital Camera
Scene Type                    : Directly photographed
Custom Rendered               : Normal
Exposure Mode                 : Auto
Digital Zoom Ratio            : 0
Focal Length In 35mm Format   : 24 mm
Scene Capture Type            : Standard
Gain Control                  : High gain up
Contrast                      : Normal
Saturation                    : Normal
Sharpness                     : Normal
PrintIM Version               : 0250
Compression                   : JPEG (old-style)
Thumbnail Offset              : 10752
Thumbnail Length              : 4470
Image Width                   : 3648
Image Height                  : 2736
Encoding Process              : Baseline DCT, Huffman coding
Bits Per Sample               : 8
Color Components              : 3
Y Cb Cr Sub Sampling          : YCbCr4:2:2 (2 1)
Advanced Scene Mode           : Off
Aperture                      : 2.0
Blue Balance                  : 2.579696
Image Size                    : 3648x2736
Megapixels                    : 10.0
Red Balance                   : 1.213472
Scale Factor To 35 mm Equivalent: 4.7
Shutter Speed                 : 1/30
Thumbnail Image               : (Binary data 4470 bytes, use -b option to extract)
Circle Of Confusion           : 0.006 mm
Field Of View                 : 73.7 deg
Focal Length                  : 5.1 mm (35 mm equivalent: 24.0 mm)
Hyperfocal Distance           : 2.04 m
Light Value                   : 5.2
```

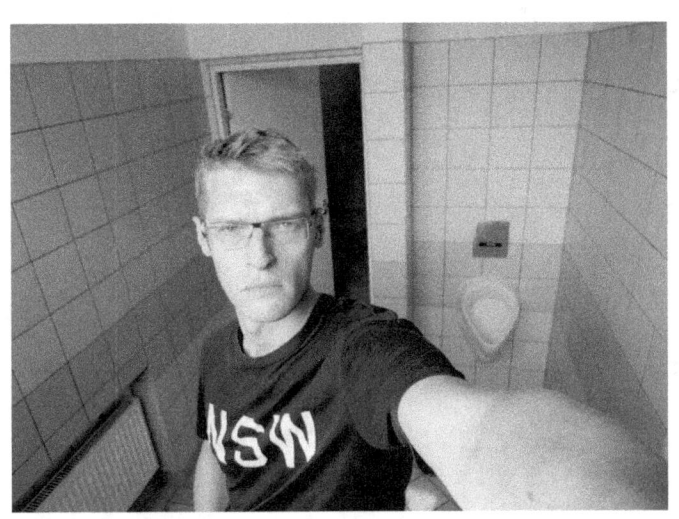

```
ExifTool Version Number         : 10.05
File Name                       : P1000844.RW2
Directory                       : ../Selection
File Size                       : 12 MB
File Modification Date/Time     : 2009:08:22 13:30:32+02:00
File Access Date/Time           : 2015:11:29 14:04:38+01:00
File Inode Change Date/Time     : 2015:11:05 21:35:08+01:00
File Permissions                : rwxr-xr-x
File Type                       : RW2
File Type Extension             : rw2
MIME Type                       : image/x-panasonic-rw2
Exif Byte Order                 : Little-endian (Intel, II)
Panasonic Raw Version           : 0300
Sensor Width                    : 3724
Sensor Height                   : 2754
Sensor Top Border               : 6
Sensor Left Border              : 8
Sensor Bottom Border            : 2742
Sensor Right Border             : 3656
Black Level 1                   : 1
Black Level 2                   : 4
Black Level 3                   : 12
Linearity Limit Red             : 4095
Linearity Limit Green           : 4095
Linearity Limit Blue            : 4095
ISO                             : 80
High ISO Multiplier Red         : 0
High ISO Multiplier Green       : 0
High ISO Multiplier Blue        : 0
Black Level Red                 : 0
Black Level Green               : 0
Black Level Blue                : 0
WB Red Level                    : 567
WB Green Level                  : 263
WB Blue Level                   : 410
Num WB Entries                  : 7
WB Type 1                       : Fine Weather
WB RGB Levels 1                 : 541 256 405
WB Type 2                       : Cloudy
WB RGB Levels 2                 : 593 256 377
WB Type 3                       : Shade
WB RGB Levels 3                 : 660 256 346
WB Type 4                       : Tungsten (Incandescent)
WB RGB Levels 4                 : 361 256 573
WB Type 5                       : Flash
WB RGB Levels 5                 : 613 256 367
WB Type 6                       : D55
WB RGB Levels 6                 : 556 256 410
WB Type 7                       : ISO Studio Tungsten
WB RGB Levels 7                 : 361 256 573
X Resolution                    : 180
Y Resolution                    : 180
Resolution Unit                 : inches
Software                        : Ver.1.0
Modify Date                     : 2009:08:22 13:30:33
Y Cb Cr Positioning             : Co-sited
Components Configuration        : Y, Cb, Cr, -
Compressed Bits Per Pixel       : 2
Light Source                    : Unknown
Image Quality                   : Raw
Firmware Version                : 0.1.0.0
White Balance                   : Auto
Focus Mode                      : Manual
AF Area Mode                    : 1-area
Image Stabilization             : On, Mode 2
Macro Mode                      : Off
Shooting Mode                   : Program
Audio                           : No
Data Dump                       : (Binary data 8200 bytes, use -b option to extract)
Flash Bias                      : 0
Internal Serial Number          : (F37) 2008:09:24 no. 0023
Panasonic Exif Version          : 0270
Color Effect                    : Off
Time Since Power On             : 00:01:06.76
Burst Mode                      : Off
Sequence Number                 : 0
Contrast Mode                   : Normal
Noise Reduction                 : Standard
Self Timer                      : Off
Rotation                        : Horizontal (normal)
AF Assist Lamp                  : Enabled but Not Used
Color Mode                      : Normal
Baby Age                        : (not set)
Optical Zoom Mode               : Standard
Conversion Lens                 : Off
Travel Day                      : n/a
```

```
Contrast                       : Normal
World Time Location            : Home
Text Stamp                     : Off
Program ISO                    : n/a
Advanced Scene Type            : 1
Faces Detected                 : 0
Saturation                     : Normal
Sharpness                      : Normal
Film Mode                      : Standard (color)
Color Temp Kelvin              : 0
WB Shift AB                    : 0
WB Shift GM                    : 0
Flash Curtain                  : n/a
Panasonic Image Width          : 3648
Panasonic Image Height         : 2736
AF Point Position              : none
Num Face Positions             : 0
Maker Note Version             : 0130
Scene Mode                     : Off
Flash Fired                    : No
Flashpix Version               : 0100
Color Space                    : sRGB
Exif Image Width               : 1920
Exif Image Height              : 1440
Interoperability Index         : R98 - DCF basic file (sRGB)
Interoperability Version       : 0100
Sensing Method                 : One-chip color area
Scene Type                     : Directly photographed
Custom Rendered                : Normal
Exposure Mode                  : Auto
Digital Zoom Ratio             : 0
Focal Length In 35mm Format    : 24 mm
Scene Capture Type             : Standard
Gain Control                   : None
PrintIM Version                : 0250
Compression                    : JPEG (old-style)
Thumbnail Offset               : 12288
Thumbnail Length               : 4698
Encoding Process               : Baseline DCT, Huffman coding
Bits Per Sample                : 8
Color Components               : 3
Y Cb Cr Sub Sampling           : YCbCr4:2:2 (2 1)
Jpg From Raw                   : (Binary data 485888 bytes, use -b option to extract)
Make                           : Panasonic
Camera Model Name              : DMC-LX3
Strip Offsets                  : 4294967295
Orientation                    : Horizontal (normal)
Rows Per Strip                 : 2754
Strip Byte Counts              : 20511792
Raw Data Offset                : 487424
Distortion Param 02            : 0.010772705078125
Distortion Param 04            : 0.02056884765625
Distortion Scale               : 1
Distortion Correction          : On
Distortion Param 08            : 0.12359619140625
Distortion Param 09            : 0.00579833984375
Distortion Param 11            : -0.02374267578125
Exposure Time                  : 1/125
F Number                       : 2.0
Exposure Program               : Program AE
Exif Version                   : 0221
Date/Time Original             : 2009:08:22 13:30:33
Create Date                    : 2009:08:22 13:30:33
Exposure Compensation          : 0
Max Aperture Value             : 2.0
Metering Mode                  : Multi-segment
Flash                          : Off, Did not fire
Focal Length                   : 5.1 mm
File Source                    : Digital Camera
Advanced Scene Mode            : Off
Aperture                       : 2.0
Blue Balance                   : 1.558935
Image Height                   : 2736
Image Width                    : 3648
Red Balance                    : 2.155894
Scale Factor To 35 mm Equivalent: 4.7
Shutter Speed                  : 1/125
Thumbnail Image                : (Binary data 4698 bytes, use -b option to extract)
Circle Of Confusion            : 0.006 mm
Field Of View                  : 73.7 deg
Focal Length                   : 5.1 mm (35 mm equivalent: 24.0 mm)
Hyperfocal Distance            : 2.04 m
Image Size                     : 3648x2736
Light Value                    : 9.3
Megapixels                     : 10.0
```

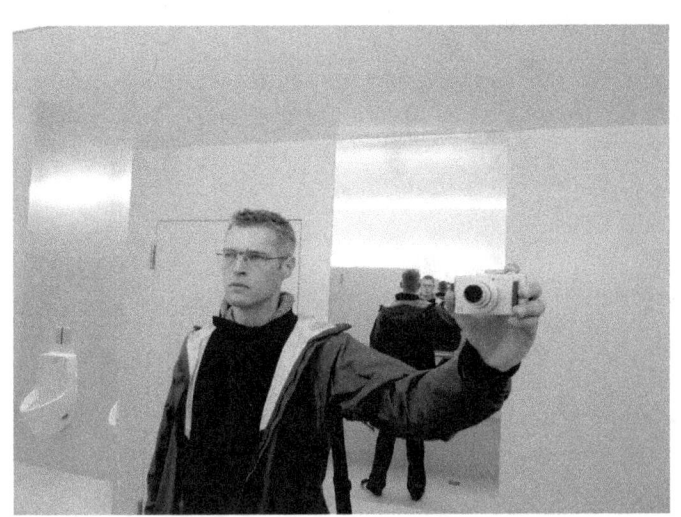

```
ExifTool Version Number         : 10.05
File Name                       : P1010080.JPG
Directory                       : ../Selection
File Size                       : 2.7 MB
File Modification Date/Time     : 2009:10:25 13:18:26+01:00
File Access Date/Time           : 2015:11:29 14:04:38+01:00
File Inode Change Date/Time     : 2015:11:05 21:35:08+01:00
File Permissions                : rw-r--r--
File Type                       : JPEG
File Type Extension             : jpg
MIME Type                       : image/jpeg
Exif Byte Order                 : Little-endian (Intel, II)
Make                            : Panasonic
Camera Model Name               : DMC-LX3
Orientation                     : Horizontal (normal)
X Resolution                    : 180
Y Resolution                    : 180
Resolution Unit                 : inches
Software                        : Ver.1.0
Modify Date                     : 2009:10:25 13:18:26
Y Cb Cr Positioning             : Co-sited
Exposure Time                   : 1/30
F Number                        : 2.0
Exposure Program                : Program AE
ISO                             : 80
Exif Version                    : 0221
Date/Time Original              : 2009:10:25 13:18:26
Create Date                     : 2009:10:25 13:18:26
Components Configuration        : Y, Cb, Cr, -
Compressed Bits Per Pixel       : 4
Exposure Compensation           : 0
Max Aperture Value              : 2.0
Metering Mode                   : Multi-segment
Light Source                    : Unknown
Flash                           : Off, Did not fire
Focal Length                    : 5.1 mm
Image Quality                   : High
Firmware Version                : 0.1.0.0
White Balance                   : Auto
Focus Mode                      : Auto
AF Area Mode                    : 5-area
Image Stabilization             : On, Mode 2
Macro Mode                      : Off
Shooting Mode                   : Program
Audio                           : No
Data Dump                       : (Binary data 8200 bytes, use -b option to extract)
Flash Bias                      : 0
Internal Serial Number          : (F37) 2008:09:24 no. 0023
Panasonic Exif Version          : 0270
Color Effect                    : Off
Time Since Power On             : 00:00:17.39
Burst Mode                      : Off
Sequence Number                 : 0
Contrast Mode                   : Normal
Noise Reduction                 : Standard
Self Timer                      : Off
Rotation                        : Horizontal (normal)
AF Assist Lamp                  : Enabled but Not Used
Color Mode                      : Normal
Optical Zoom Mode               : Standard
Conversion Lens                 : Off
Travel Day                      : n/a
World Time Location             : Home
Program ISO                     : n/a
Advanced Scene Type             : 1
Faces Detected                  : 1
Film Mode                       : Standard (color)
Color Temp Kelvin               : 0
WB Shift AB                     : 0
WB Shift GM                     : 0
Flash Curtain                   : n/a
Panasonic Image Width           : 0
Panasonic Image Height          : 0
AF Point Position               : 0.5 0.5
Num Face Positions              : 1
Face 1 Position                 : 70 108 29 29
Maker Note Version              : 0130
Scene Mode                      : Off
WB Red Level                    : 1931
WB Green Level                  : 1054
WB Blue Level                   : 2215
Flash Fired                     : No
Text Stamp                      : Off
Baby Age                        : (not set)
Flashpix Version                : 0100
Color Space                     : sRGB
```

```
Exif Image Width               : 3648
Exif Image Height              : 2736
Interoperability Index         : R98 - DCF basic file (sRGB)
Interoperability Version       : 0100
Sensing Method                 : One-chip color area
File Source                    : Digital Camera
Scene Type                     : Directly photographed
Custom Rendered                : Normal
Exposure Mode                  : Auto
Digital Zoom Ratio             : 0
Focal Length In 35mm Format    : 24 mm
Scene Capture Type             : Standard
Gain Control                   : None
Contrast                       : Normal
Saturation                     : Normal
Sharpness                      : Normal
PrintIM Version                : 0250
Compression                    : JPEG (old-style)
Thumbnail Offset               : 10752
Thumbnail Length               : 3916
Image Width                    : 3648
Image Height                   : 2736
Encoding Process               : Baseline DCT, Huffman coding
Bits Per Sample                : 8
Color Components               : 3
Y Cb Cr Sub Sampling           : YCbCr4:2:2 (2 1)
Advanced Scene Mode            : Off
Aperture                       : 2.0
Blue Balance                   : 2.101518
Image Size                     : 3648x2736
Megapixels                     : 10.0
Red Balance                    : 1.832068
Scale Factor To 35 mm Equivalent: 4.7
Shutter Speed                  : 1/30
Thumbnail Image                : (Binary data 3916 bytes, use -b option to extract)
Circle Of Confusion            : 0.006 mm
Field Of View                  : 73.7 deg
Focal Length                   : 5.1 mm (35 mm equivalent: 24.0 mm)
Hyperfocal Distance            : 2.04 m
Light Value                    : 7.2
```

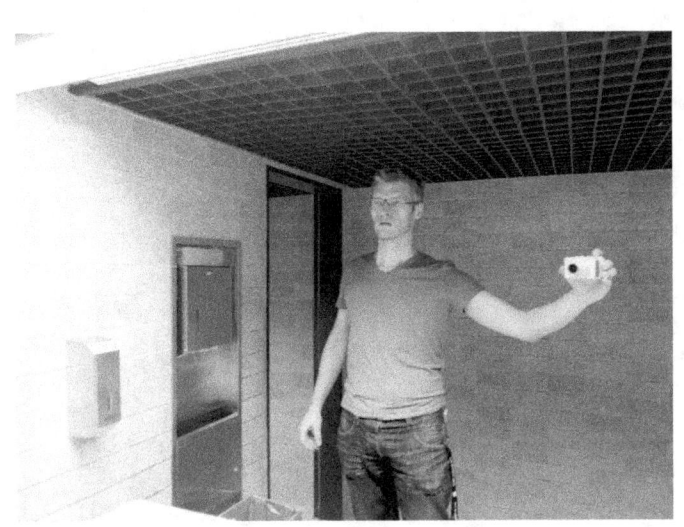

```
ExifTool Version Number         : 10.05
File Name                       : P1020197.RW2
Directory                       : ../Selection
File Size                       : 12 MB
File Modification Date/Time     : 2010:06:05 13:30:52+02:00
File Access Date/Time           : 2015:11:29 14:04:38+01:00
File Inode Change Date/Time     : 2015:11:05 21:35:08+01:00
File Permissions                : rwxr-xr-x
File Type                       : RW2
File Type Extension             : rw2
MIME Type                       : image/x-panasonic-rw2
Exif Byte Order                 : Little-endian (Intel, II)
Panasonic Raw Version           : 0310
Sensor Width                    : 3724
Sensor Height                   : 2754
Sensor Top Border               : 6
Sensor Left Border              : 8
Sensor Bottom Border            : 2742
Sensor Right Border             : 3656
Black Level 1                   : 1
Black Level 2                   : 4
Black Level 3                   : 12
Linearity Limit Red             : 4095
Linearity Limit Green           : 4095
Linearity Limit Blue            : 4095
ISO                             : 400
High ISO Multiplier Red         : 0
High ISO Multiplier Green       : 0
High ISO Multiplier Blue        : 0
Black Level Red                 : 0
Black Level Green               : 0
Black Level Blue                : 0
WB Red Level                    : 486
WB Green Level                  : 263
WB Blue Level                   : 604
Num WB Entries                  : 7
WB Type 1                       : Fine Weather
WB RGB Levels 1                 : 541 256 405
WB Type 2                       : Cloudy
WB RGB Levels 2                 : 601 256 374
WB Type 3                       : Shade
WB RGB Levels 3                 : 666 256 343
WB Type 4                       : Tungsten (Incandescent)
WB RGB Levels 4                 : 361 256 573
WB Type 5                       : Flash
WB RGB Levels 5                 : 613 256 367
WB Type 6                       : D55
WB RGB Levels 6                 : 556 256 410
WB Type 7                       : ISO Studio Tungsten
WB RGB Levels 7                 : 361 256 573
X Resolution                    : 180
Y Resolution                    : 180
Resolution Unit                 : inches
Software                        : Ver.2.1
Modify Date                     : 2010:06:05 13:30:52
Artist                          :
Y Cb Cr Positioning             : Co-sited
Components Configuration        : Y, Cb, Cr, -
Compressed Bits Per Pixel       : 4
Light Source                    : Unknown
Image Quality                   : Raw
Firmware Version                : 0.2.1.0
White Balance                   : Auto
Focus Mode                      : Auto
AF Area Mode                    : 5-area
Image Stabilization             : On, Mode 2
Macro Mode                      : Off
Shooting Mode                   : Program
Audio                           : No
Data Dump                       : (Binary data 8200 bytes, use -b option to extract)
Flash Bias                      : 0
Internal Serial Number          : (F37) 2008:09:24 no. 0023
Panasonic Exif Version          : 0291
Color Effect                    : Off
Time Since Power On             : 00:00:13.48
Burst Mode                      : Off
Sequence Number                 : 0
Contrast Mode                   : Normal
Noise Reduction                 : Standard
Self Timer                      : Off
Rotation                        : Horizontal (normal)
AF Assist Lamp                  : Enabled but Not Used
Color Mode                      : Normal
Baby Age                        : (not set)
Optical Zoom Mode               : Standard
Conversion Lens                 : Off
```

Travel Day	: n/a
Contrast	: Normal
World Time Location	: Home
Text Stamp	: Off
Program ISO	: n/a
Advanced Scene Type	: 1
Faces Detected	: 0
Saturation	: Normal
Sharpness	: Normal
Film Mode	: Standard (color)
Color Temp Kelvin	: 0
WB Shift AB	: 0
WB Shift GM	: 0
Flash Curtain	: n/a
Panasonic Image Width	: 3648
Panasonic Image Height	: 2736
AF Point Position	: 0.5 0.5
Num Face Positions	: 0
Maker Note Version	: 0132
Scene Mode	: Off
Flash Fired	: No
Flashpix Version	: 0100
Color Space	: sRGB
Exif Image Width	: 1920
Exif Image Height	: 1440
Interoperability Index	: R98 - DCF basic file (sRGB)
Interoperability Version	: 0100
Sensing Method	: One-chip color area
Scene Type	: Directly photographed
Custom Rendered	: Normal
Exposure Mode	: Auto
Digital Zoom Ratio	: 0
Focal Length In 35mm Format	: 28 mm
Scene Capture Type	: Standard
Gain Control	: High gain up
PrintIM Version	: 0250
Compression	: JPEG (old-style)
Thumbnail Offset	: 12288
Thumbnail Length	: 4782
Encoding Process	: Baseline DCT, Huffman coding
Bits Per Sample	: 8
Color Components	: 3
Y Cb Cr Sub Sampling	: YCbCr4:2:2 (2 1)
Jpg From Raw	: (Binary data 666624 bytes, use -b option to extract)
Make	: Panasonic
Camera Model Name	: DMC-LX3
Strip Offsets	: 4294967295
Orientation	: Horizontal (normal)
Rows Per Strip	: 2754
Strip Byte Counts	: 20511792
Raw Data Offset	: 668160
Distortion Param 02	: 0.001220703125
Distortion Param 04	: 0.00762939453125
Distortion Scale	: 1
Distortion Correction	: On
Distortion Param 08	: 0.099365234375
Distortion Param 09	: 0.011077880859375
Distortion Param 11	: -0.006195068359375
Exposure Time	: 1/40
F Number	: 2.1
Exposure Program	: Program AE
Exif Version	: 0221
Date/Time Original	: 2010:06:05 13:30:52
Create Date	: 2010:06:05 13:30:52
Exposure Compensation	: 0
Max Aperture Value	: 2.0
Metering Mode	: Multi-segment
Flash	: Off, Did not fire
Focal Length	: 5.9 mm
File Source	: Digital Camera
Advanced Scene Mode	: Off
Aperture	: 2.1
Blue Balance	: 2.296578
Image Height	: 2736
Image Width	: 3648
Red Balance	: 1.847909
Scale Factor To 35 mm Equivalent	: 4.7
Shutter Speed	: 1/40
Thumbnail Image	: (Binary data 4782 bytes, use -b option to extract)
Circle Of Confusion	: 0.006 mm
Field Of View	: 65.5 deg
Focal Length	: 5.9 mm (35 mm equivalent: 28.0 mm)
Hyperfocal Distance	: 2.62 m
Image Size	: 3648x2736
Light Value	: 5.5
Megapixels	: 10.0

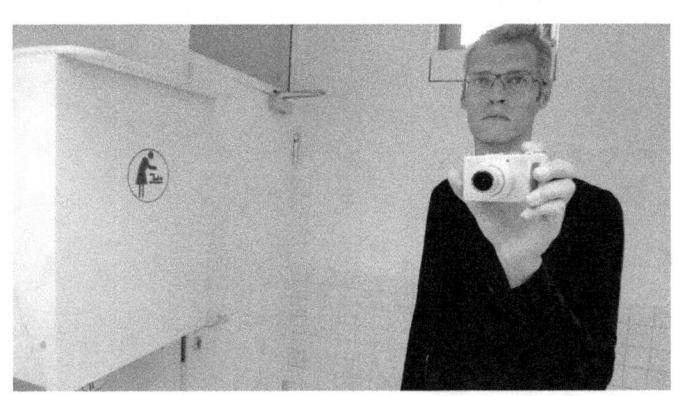

```
ExifTool Version Number         : 10.05
File Name                       : P1020395.JPG
Directory                       : ../Selection
File Size                       : 2.8 MB
File Modification Date/Time     : 2010:08:12 21:44:16+02:00
File Access Date/Time           : 2015:11:29 14:04:39+01:00
File Inode Change Date/Time     : 2015:11:05 21:35:08+01:00
File Permissions                : rwxr-xr-x
File Type                       : JPEG
File Type Extension             : jpg
MIME Type                       : image/jpeg
Exif Byte Order                 : Little-endian (Intel, II)
Make                            : Panasonic
Camera Model Name               : DMC-LX3
Orientation                     : Horizontal (normal)
X Resolution                    : 180
Y Resolution                    : 180
Resolution Unit                 : inches
Software                        : Ver.2.1
Modify Date                     : 2010:08:12 12:44:16
Artist                          :
Y Cb Cr Positioning             : Co-sited
Exposure Time                   : 1/30
F Number                        : 2.0
Exposure Program                : Program AE
ISO                             : 125
Exif Version                    : 0221
Date/Time Original              : 2010:08:12 12:44:16
Create Date                     : 2010:08:12 12:44:16
Components Configuration        : Y, Cb, Cr, -
Compressed Bits Per Pixel       : 4
Exposure Compensation           : 0
Max Aperture Value              : 2.0
Metering Mode                   : Multi-segment
Light Source                    : Unknown
Flash                           : Off, Did not fire
Focal Length                    : 5.1 mm
Image Quality                   : High
Firmware Version                : 0.2.1.0
White Balance                   : Auto
Focus Mode                      : Auto
AF Area Mode                    : 5-area
Image Stabilization             : On, Mode 2
Macro Mode                      : Off
Shooting Mode                   : Program
Audio                           : No
Data Dump                       : (Binary data 8200 bytes, use -b option to extract)
Flash Bias                      : 0
Internal Serial Number          : (F37) 2008:09:24 no. 0023
Panasonic Exif Version          : 0291
Color Effect                    : Off
Time Since Power On             : 00:00:36.75
Burst Mode                      : Off
Sequence Number                 : 0
Contrast Mode                   : Normal
Noise Reduction                 : Standard
Self Timer                      : Off
Rotation                        : Horizontal (normal)
AF Assist Lamp                  : Enabled but Not Used
Color Mode                      : Normal
Optical Zoom Mode               : Standard
Conversion Lens                 : Off
Travel Day                      : n/a
World Time Location             : Home
Program ISO                     : n/a
Advanced Scene Type             : 1
Faces Detected                  : 1
Film Mode                       : Standard (color)
Color Temp Kelvin               : 0
WB Shift AB                     : 0
WB Shift GM                     : 0
Flash Curtain                   : n/a
Panasonic Image Width           : 0
Panasonic Image Height          : 0
AF Point Position               : 0.7 0.5
Num Face Positions              : 1
Face 1 Position                 : 233 51 29 29
Maker Note Version              : 0132
Scene Mode                      : Off
WB Red Level                    : 1874
WB Green Level                  : 1054
WB Blue Level                   : 2537
Flash Fired                     : No
Text Stamp                      : Off
Baby Age                        : (not set)
Flashpix Version                : 0100
```

Color Space	: sRGB
Exif Image Width	: 3968
Exif Image Height	: 2232
Interoperability Index	: R98 - DCF basic file (sRGB)
Interoperability Version	: 0100
Sensing Method	: One-chip color area
File Source	: Digital Camera
Scene Type	: Directly photographed
Custom Rendered	: Normal
Exposure Mode	: Auto
Digital Zoom Ratio	: 0
Focal Length In 35mm Format	: 24 mm
Scene Capture Type	: Standard
Gain Control	: Low gain up
Contrast	: Normal
Saturation	: Normal
Sharpness	: Normal
PrintIM Version	: 0250
Compression	: JPEG (old-style)
Thumbnail Offset	: 10752
Thumbnail Length	: 3927
Image Width	: 3968
Image Height	: 2232
Encoding Process	: Baseline DCT, Huffman coding
Bits Per Sample	: 8
Color Components	: 3
Y Cb Cr Sub Sampling	: YCbCr4:2:2 (2 1)
Advanced Scene Mode	: Off
Aperture	: 2.0
Blue Balance	: 2.407021
Image Size	: 3968x2232
Megapixels	: 8.9
Red Balance	: 1.777989
Scale Factor To 35 mm Equivalent: 4.7	
Shutter Speed	: 1/30
Thumbnail Image	: (Binary data 3927 bytes, use -b option to extract)
Circle Of Confusion	: 0.006 mm
Field Of View	: 73.7 deg
Focal Length	: 5.1 mm (35 mm equivalent: 24.0 mm)
Hyperfocal Distance	: 2.04 m
Light Value	: 6.6

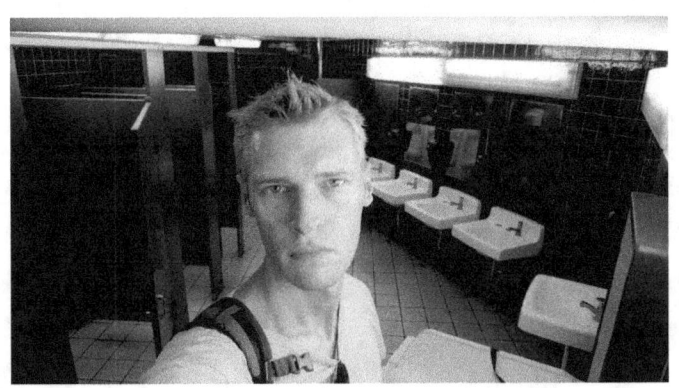

```
ExifTool Version Number         : 10.05
File Name                       : P1020537.RW2
Directory                       : ../Selection
File Size                       : 10 MB
File Modification Date/Time     : 2010:08:23 05:49:50+02:00
File Access Date/Time           : 2015:11:29 14:04:39+01:00
File Inode Change Date/Time     : 2015:11:05 21:35:08+01:00
File Permissions                : rwxr-xr-x
File Type                       : RW2
File Type Extension             : rw2
MIME Type                       : image/x-panasonic-rw2
Exif Byte Order                 : Little-endian (Intel, II)
Panasonic Raw Version           : 0310
Sensor Width                    : 4060
Sensor Height                   : 2250
Sensor Top Border               : 6
Sensor Left Border              : 8
Sensor Bottom Border            : 2238
Sensor Right Border             : 3976
Black Level 1                   : 1
Black Level 2                   : 4
Black Level 3                   : 12
Linearity Limit Red             : 4095
Linearity Limit Green           : 4095
Linearity Limit Blue            : 4095
ISO                             : 250
High ISO Multiplier Red         : 0
High ISO Multiplier Green       : 0
High ISO Multiplier Blue        : 0
Black Level Red                 : 0
Black Level Green               : 0
Black Level Blue                : 0
WB Red Level                    : 378
WB Green Level                  : 263
WB Blue Level                   : 674
Num WB Entries                  : 7
WB Type 1                       : Fine Weather
WB RGB Levels 1                 : 541 256 405
WB Type 2                       : Cloudy
WB RGB Levels 2                 : 601 256 374
WB Type 3                       : Shade
WB RGB Levels 3                 : 666 256 343
WB Type 4                       : Tungsten (Incandescent)
WB RGB Levels 4                 : 361 256 573
WB Type 5                       : Flash
WB RGB Levels 5                 : 613 256 367
WB Type 6                       : D55
WB RGB Levels 6                 : 556 256 410
WB Type 7                       : ISO Studio Tungsten
WB RGB Levels 7                 : 361 256 573
X Resolution                    : 180
Y Resolution                    : 180
Resolution Unit                 : inches
Software                        : Ver.2.1
Modify Date                     : 2010:08:22 20:49:50
Artist                          :
Y Cb Cr Positioning             : Co-sited
Components Configuration        : Y, Cb, Cr, -
Compressed Bits Per Pixel       : 0
Light Source                    : Unknown
Image Quality                   : Raw
Firmware Version                : 0.2.1.0
White Balance                   : Auto
Focus Mode                      : Auto
AF Area Mode                    : 5-area
Image Stabilization             : On, Mode 2
Macro Mode                      : Off
Shooting Mode                   : Program
Audio                           : No
Data Dump                       : (Binary data 8200 bytes, use -b option to extract)
Flash Bias                      : 0
Internal Serial Number          : (F37) 2008:09:24 no. 0023
Panasonic Exif Version          : 0291
Color Effect                    : Off
Time Since Power On             : 00:00:11.41
Burst Mode                      : Off
Sequence Number                 : 0
Contrast Mode                   : Normal
Noise Reduction                 : Standard
Self Timer                      : Off
Rotation                        : Horizontal (normal)
AF Assist Lamp                  : Enabled but Not Used
Color Mode                      : Normal
Baby Age                        : (not set)
Optical Zoom Mode               : Standard
Conversion Lens                 : Off
```

```
Travel Day                            : n/a
Contrast                              : Normal
World Time Location                   : Home
Text Stamp                            : Off
Program ISO                           : n/a
Advanced Scene Type                   : 1
Faces Detected                        : 0
Saturation                            : Normal
Sharpness                             : Normal
Film Mode                             : Standard (color)
Color Temp Kelvin                     : 0
WB Shift AB                           : 0
WB Shift GM                           : 0
Flash Curtain                         : n/a
Panasonic Image Width                 : 3968
Panasonic Image Height                : 2232
AF Point Position                     : 0.5 0.5
Num Face Positions                    : 0
Maker Note Version                    : 0132
Scene Mode                            : Off
Flash Fired                           : No
Flashpix Version                      : 0100
Color Space                           : sRGB
Exif Image Width                      : 1920
Exif Image Height                     : 1080
Interoperability Index                : R98 - DCF basic file (sRGB)
Interoperability Version              : 0100
Sensing Method                        : One-chip color area
Scene Type                            : Directly photographed
Custom Rendered                       : Normal
Exposure Mode                         : Auto
Digital Zoom Ratio                    : 0
Focal Length In 35mm Format           : 24 mm
Scene Capture Type                    : Standard
Gain Control                          : High gain up
PrintIM Version                       : 0250
Compression                           : JPEG (old-style)
Thumbnail Offset                      : 12288
Thumbnail Length                      : 5633
Encoding Process                      : Baseline DCT, Huffman coding
Bits Per Sample                       : 8
Color Components                      : 3
Y Cb Cr Sub Sampling                  : YCbCr4:2:2 (2 1)
Jpg From Raw                          : (Binary data 449536 bytes, use -b option to extract)
Make                                  : Panasonic
Camera Model Name                     : DMC-LX3
Strip Offsets                         : 4294967295
Orientation                           : Horizontal (normal)
Rows Per Strip                        : 2250
Strip Byte Counts                     : 18270000
Raw Data Offset                       : 451072
Distortion Param 02                   : 0.010772705078125
Distortion Param 04                   : 0.02056884765625
Distortion Scale                      : 1
Distortion Correction                 : On
Distortion Param 08                   : 0.12359619140625
Distortion Param 09                   : 0.00579833984375
Distortion Param 11                   : -0.02374267578125
Exposure Time                         : 1/60
F Number                              : 2.0
Exposure Program                      : Program AE
Exif Version                          : 0221
Date/Time Original                    : 2010:08:22 20:49:50
Create Date                           : 2010:08:22 20:49:50
Exposure Compensation                 : 0
Max Aperture Value                    : 2.0
Metering Mode                         : Multi-segment
Flash                                 : Off, Did not fire
Focal Length                          : 5.1 mm
File Source                           : Digital Camera
Advanced Scene Mode                   : Off
Aperture                              : 2.0
Blue Balance                          : 2.562738
Image Height                          : 2232
Image Width                           : 3968
Red Balance                           : 1.437262
Scale Factor To 35 mm Equivalent: 4.7
Shutter Speed                         : 1/60
Thumbnail Image                       : (Binary data 5633 bytes, use -b option to extract)
Circle Of Confusion                   : 0.006 mm
Field Of View                         : 73.7 deg
Focal Length                          : 5.1 mm (35 mm equivalent: 24.0 mm)
Hyperfocal Distance                   : 2.04 m
Image Size                            : 3968x2232
Light Value                           : 6.6
Megapixels                            : 8.9
```

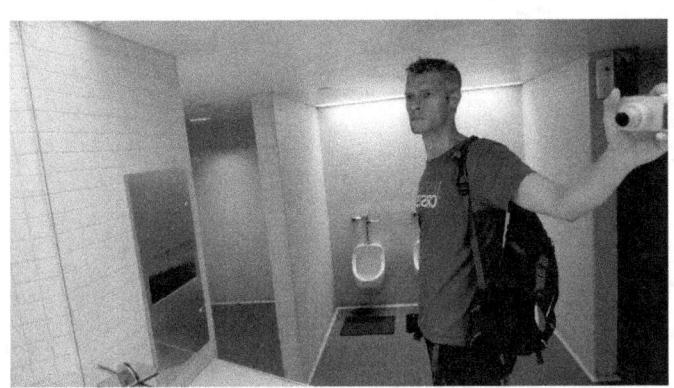

```
ExifTool Version Number         : 10.05
File Name                       : P1020552.JPG
Directory                       : ../Selection
File Size                       : 3.1 MB
File Modification Date/Time     : 2010:08:25 12:20:26+02:00
File Access Date/Time           : 2015:11:29 14:04:39+01:00
File Inode Change Date/Time     : 2015:11:05 21:35:08+01:00
File Permissions                : rwxr-xr-x
File Type                       : JPEG
File Type Extension             : jpg
MIME Type                       : image/jpeg
Exif Byte Order                 : Little-endian (Intel, II)
Make                            : Panasonic
Camera Model Name               : DMC-LX3
Orientation                     : Horizontal (normal)
X Resolution                    : 180
Y Resolution                    : 180
Resolution Unit                 : inches
Software                        : Ver.2.1
Modify Date                     : 2010:08:25 03:20:27
Artist                          :
Y Cb Cr Positioning             : Co-sited
Exposure Time                   : 1/60
F Number                        : 2.0
Exposure Program                : Program AE
ISO                             : 400
Exif Version                    : 0221
Date/Time Original              : 2010:08:25 03:20:27
Create Date                     : 2010:08:25 03:20:27
Components Configuration        : Y, Cb, Cr, -
Compressed Bits Per Pixel       : 4
Exposure Compensation           : 0
Max Aperture Value              : 2.0
Metering Mode                   : Multi-segment
Light Source                    : Unknown
Flash                           : Off, Did not fire
Focal Length                    : 5.1 mm
Image Quality                   : High
Firmware Version                : 0.2.1.0
White Balance                   : Auto
Focus Mode                      : Auto
AF Area Mode                    : 5-area
Image Stabilization             : On, Mode 2
Macro Mode                      : Off
Shooting Mode                   : Program
Audio                           : No
Data Dump                       : (Binary data 8200 bytes, use -b option to extract)
Flash Bias                      : 0
Internal Serial Number          : (F37) 2008:09:24 no. 0023
Panasonic Exif Version          : 0291
Color Effect                    : Off
Time Since Power On             : 00:00:22.03
Burst Mode                      : Off
Sequence Number                 : 0
Contrast Mode                   : Normal
Noise Reduction                 : Standard
Self Timer                      : Off
Rotation                        : Horizontal (normal)
AF Assist Lamp                  : Enabled but Not Used
Color Mode                      : Normal
Optical Zoom Mode               : Standard
Conversion Lens                 : Off
Travel Day                      : n/a
World Time Location             : Home
Program ISO                     : n/a
Advanced Scene Type             : 1
Faces Detected                  : 0
Film Mode                       : Standard (color)
Color Temp Kelvin               : 0
WB Shift AB                     : 0
WB Shift GM                     : 0
Flash Curtain                   : n/a
Panasonic Image Width           : 0
Panasonic Image Height          : 0
AF Point Position               : 0.5 0.5
Num Face Positions              : 0
Maker Note Version              : 0132
Scene Mode                      : Off
WB Red Level                    : 1906
WB Green Level                  : 1054
WB Blue Level                   : 2618
Flash Fired                     : No
Text Stamp                      : Off
Baby Age                        : (not set)
Flashpix Version                : 0100
Color Space                     : sRGB
```

```
Exif Image Width              : 3968
Exif Image Height             : 2232
Interoperability Index        : R98 - DCF basic file (sRGB)
Interoperability Version      : 0100
Sensing Method                : One-chip color area
File Source                   : Digital Camera
Scene Type                    : Directly photographed
Custom Rendered               : Normal
Exposure Mode                 : Auto
Digital Zoom Ratio            : 0
Focal Length In 35mm Format   : 24 mm
Scene Capture Type            : Standard
Gain Control                  : High gain up
Contrast                      : Normal
Saturation                    : Normal
Sharpness                     : Normal
PrintIM Version               : 0250
Compression                   : JPEG (old-style)
Thumbnail Offset              : 10752
Thumbnail Length              : 4542
Image Width                   : 3968
Image Height                  : 2232
Encoding Process              : Baseline DCT, Huffman coding
Bits Per Sample               : 8
Color Components              : 3
Y Cb Cr Sub Sampling          : YCbCr4:2:2 (2 1)
Advanced Scene Mode           : Off
Aperture                      : 2.0
Blue Balance                  : 2.483871
Image Size                    : 3968x2232
Megapixels                    : 8.9
Red Balance                   : 1.808349
Scale Factor To 35 mm Equivalent: 4.7
Shutter Speed                 : 1/60
Thumbnail Image               : (Binary data 4542 bytes, use -b option to extract)
Circle Of Confusion           : 0.006 mm
Field Of View                 : 73.7 deg
Focal Length                  : 5.1 mm (35 mm equivalent: 24.0 mm)
Hyperfocal Distance           : 2.04 m
Light Value                   : 5.9
```

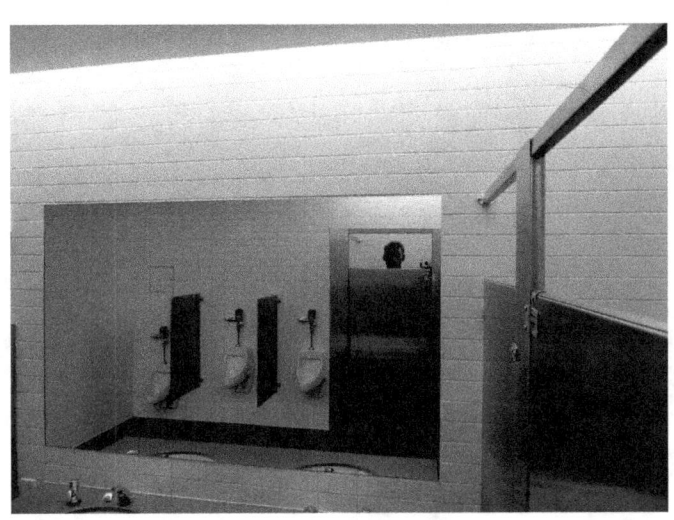

```
ExifTool Version Number         : 10.05
File Name                       : P1020675.JPG
Directory                       : ../Selection
File Size                       : 3.5 MB
File Modification Date/Time     : 2010:09:05 08:06:54+02:00
File Access Date/Time           : 2015:11:29 14:04:39+01:00
File Inode Change Date/Time     : 2015:11:05 21:35:08+01:00
File Permissions                : rwxr-xr-x
File Type                       : JPEG
File Type Extension             : jpg
MIME Type                       : image/jpeg
Exif Byte Order                 : Little-endian (Intel, II)
Make                            : Panasonic
Camera Model Name               : DMC-LX3
Orientation                     : Horizontal (normal)
X Resolution                    : 180
Y Resolution                    : 180
Resolution Unit                 : inches
Software                        : Ver.2.1
Modify Date                     : 2010:09:04 23:06:54
Artist                          :
Y Cb Cr Positioning             : Co-sited
Exposure Time                   : 1/50
F Number                        : 2.0
Exposure Program                : Program AE
ISO                             : 125
Exif Version                    : 0221
Date/Time Original              : 2010:09:04 23:06:54
Create Date                     : 2010:09:04 23:06:54
Components Configuration        : Y, Cb, Cr, -
Compressed Bits Per Pixel       : 4
Exposure Compensation           : 0
Max Aperture Value              : 2.0
Metering Mode                   : Multi-segment
Light Source                    : Unknown
Flash                           : Off, Did not fire
Focal Length                    : 5.1 mm
Image Quality                   : High
Firmware Version                : 0.2.1.0
White Balance                   : Auto
Focus Mode                      : Auto
AF Area Mode                    : 5-area
Image Stabilization             : On, Mode 2
Macro Mode                      : Off
Shooting Mode                   : Program
Audio                           : No
Data Dump                       : (Binary data 8200 bytes, use -b option to extract)
Flash Bias                      : 0
Internal Serial Number          : (F37) 2008:09:24 no. 0023
Panasonic Exif Version          : 0291
Color Effect                    : Off
Time Since Power On             : 00:00:15.24
Burst Mode                      : Off
Sequence Number                 : 0
Contrast Mode                   : Normal
Noise Reduction                 : Standard
Self Timer                      : Off
Rotation                        : Horizontal (normal)
AF Assist Lamp                  : Enabled but Not Used
Color Mode                      : Normal
Optical Zoom Mode               : Standard
Conversion Lens                 : Off
Travel Day                      : n/a
World Time Location             : Home
Program ISO                     : n/a
Advanced Scene Type             : 1
Faces Detected                  : 0
Film Mode                       : Standard (color)
Color Temp Kelvin               : 0
WB Shift AB                     : 0
WB Shift GM                     : 0
Flash Curtain                   : n/a
Panasonic Image Width           : 0
Panasonic Image Height          : 0
AF Point Position               : 0.5 0.5
Num Face Positions              : 0
Maker Note Version              : 0132
Scene Mode                      : Off
WB Red Level                    : 1520
WB Green Level                  : 1054
WB Blue Level                   : 2726
Flash Fired                     : No
Text Stamp                      : Off
Baby Age                        : (not set)
Flashpix Version                : 0100
Color Space                     : sRGB
```

```
Exif Image Width              : 3648
Exif Image Height             : 2736
Interoperability Index        : R98 - DCF basic file (sRGB)
Interoperability Version      : 0100
Sensing Method                : One-chip color area
File Source                   : Digital Camera
Scene Type                    : Directly photographed
Custom Rendered               : Normal
Exposure Mode                 : Auto
Digital Zoom Ratio            : 0
Focal Length In 35mm Format   : 24 mm
Scene Capture Type            : Standard
Gain Control                  : Low gain up
Contrast                      : Normal
Saturation                    : Normal
Sharpness                     : Normal
PrintIM Version               : 0250
Compression                   : JPEG (old-style)
Thumbnail Offset              : 10752
Thumbnail Length              : 4150
Image Width                   : 3648
Image Height                  : 2736
Encoding Process              : Baseline DCT, Huffman coding
Bits Per Sample               : 8
Color Components              : 3
Y Cb Cr Sub Sampling          : YCbCr4:2:2 (2 1)
Advanced Scene Mode           : Off
Aperture                      : 2.0
Blue Balance                  : 2.586338
Image Size                    : 3648x2736
Megapixels                    : 10.0
Red Balance                   : 1.442125
Scale Factor To 35 mm Equivalent: 4.7
Shutter Speed                 : 1/50
Thumbnail Image               : (Binary data 4150 bytes, use -b option to extract)
Circle Of Confusion           : 0.006 mm
Field Of View                 : 73.7 deg
Focal Length                  : 5.1 mm (35 mm equivalent: 24.0 mm)
Hyperfocal Distance           : 2.04 m
Light Value                   : 7.3
```

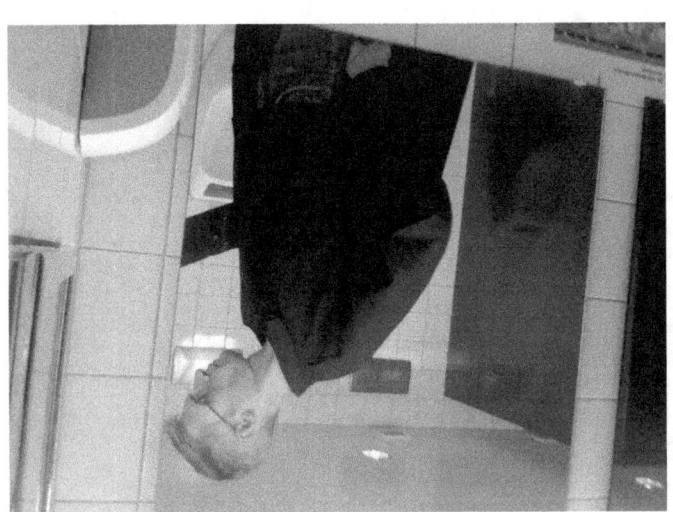

```
ExifTool Version Number        : 10.05
File Name                      : IMG_0660.JPG
Directory                      : ../Selection
File Size                      : 641 kB
File Modification Date/Time    : 2010:09:30 22:16:46+02:00
File Access Date/Time          : 2015:11:29 14:04:40+01:00
File Inode Change Date/Time    : 2015:11:05 21:35:08+01:00
File Permissions               : rw-------
File Type                      : JPEG
File Type Extension            : jpg
MIME Type                      : image/jpeg
Exif Byte Order                : Big-endian (Motorola, MM)
Make                           : Apple
Camera Model Name              : iPhone 3G
Orientation                    : Rotate 180
X Resolution                   : 72
Y Resolution                   : 72
Resolution Unit                : inches
Software                       : 4.1
Modify Date                    : 2010:09:30 22:16:46
Y Cb Cr Positioning            : Centered
F Number                       : 2.8
Exposure Program               : Program AE
Exif Version                   : 0221
Date/Time Original             : 2010:09:30 22:16:46
Create Date                    : 2010:09:30 22:16:46
Components Configuration       : Y, Cb, Cr, -
Aperture Value                 : 2.8
Metering Mode                  : Average
Flash                          : No flash function
Flashpix Version               : 0100
Color Space                    : sRGB
Exif Image Width               : 1600
Exif Image Height              : 1200
Sensing Method                 : One-chip color area
Exposure Mode                  : Auto
White Balance                  : Auto
Scene Capture Type             : Standard
GPS Latitude Ref               : North
GPS Longitude Ref              : East
GPS Time Stamp                 : 22:16:44.56
Compression                    : JPEG (old-style)
Thumbnail Offset               : 708
Thumbnail Length               : 7183
Image Width                    : 1600
Image Height                   : 1200
Encoding Process               : Baseline DCT, Huffman coding
Bits Per Sample                : 8
Color Components               : 3
Y Cb Cr Sub Sampling           : YCbCr4:2:0 (2 2)
Aperture                       : 2.8
GPS Latitude                   : 47 deg 23' 21.60" N
GPS Longitude                  : 8 deg 31' 17.40" E
GPS Position                   : 47 deg 23' 21.60" N, 8 deg 31' 17.40" E
Image Size                     : 1600x1200
Megapixels                     : 1.9
Thumbnail Image                : (Binary data 7183 bytes, use -b option to extract)
```

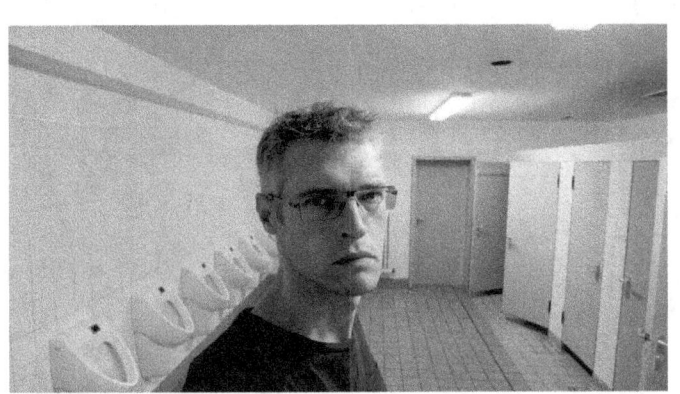

```
ExifTool Version Number         : 10.05
File Name                       : P1050278.RW2
Directory                       : ../Selection
File Size                       : 10 MB
File Modification Date/Time     : 2012:08:23 11:22:18+02:00
File Access Date/Time           : 2015:11:29 14:04:40+01:00
File Inode Change Date/Time     : 2015:11:05 21:35:08+01:00
File Permissions                : rwxrwxrwx
File Type                       : RW2
File Type Extension             : rw2
MIME Type                       : image/x-panasonic-rw2
Exif Byte Order                 : Little-endian (Intel, II)
Panasonic Raw Version           : 0310
Sensor Width                    : 4060
Sensor Height                   : 2250
Sensor Top Border               : 6
Sensor Left Border              : 8
Sensor Bottom Border            : 2238
Sensor Right Border             : 3976
Black Level 1                   : 1
Black Level 2                   : 4
Black Level 3                   : 12
Linearity Limit Red             : 4095
Linearity Limit Green           : 4095
Linearity Limit Blue            : 4095
ISO                             : 400
High ISO Multiplier Red         : 0
High ISO Multiplier Green       : 0
High ISO Multiplier Blue        : 0
Black Level Red                 : 0
Black Level Green               : 0
Black Level Blue                : 0
WB Red Level                    : 375
WB Green Level                  : 263
WB Blue Level                   : 681
Num WB Entries                  : 7
WB Type 1                       : Fine Weather
WB RGB Levels 1                 : 541 256 405
WB Type 2                       : Cloudy
WB RGB Levels 2                 : 601 256 374
WB Type 3                       : Shade
WB RGB Levels 3                 : 666 256 343
WB Type 4                       : Tungsten (Incandescent)
WB RGB Levels 4                 : 361 256 573
WB Type 5                       : Flash
WB RGB Levels 5                 : 613 256 367
WB Type 6                       : D55
WB RGB Levels 6                 : 556 256 410
WB Type 7                       : ISO Studio Tungsten
WB RGB Levels 7                 : 361 256 573
X Resolution                    : 180
Y Resolution                    : 180
Resolution Unit                 : inches
Software                        : Ver.2.2
Modify Date                     : 2012:08:23 10:22:19
Artist                          :
Y Cb Cr Positioning             : Co-sited
Components Configuration        : Y, Cb, Cr, -
Compressed Bits Per Pixel       : 0
Light Source                    : Unknown
Image Quality                   : Raw
Firmware Version                : 0.2.2.0
White Balance                   : Auto
Focus Mode                      : Auto
AF Area Mode                    : 5-area
Image Stabilization             : On, Mode 1
Macro Mode                      : Off
Shooting Mode                   : Program
Audio                           : No
Data Dump                       : (Binary data 8200 bytes, use -b option to extract)
Flash Bias                      : 0
Internal Serial Number          : (F37) 2008:09:24 no. 0023
Panasonic Exif Version          : 0291
Color Effect                    : Off
Time Since Power On             : 00:00:14.07
Burst Mode                      : Off
Sequence Number                 : 0
Contrast Mode                   : Normal
Noise Reduction                 : Standard
Self Timer                      : Off
Rotation                        : Horizontal (normal)
AF Assist Lamp                  : Disabled and Not Required
Color Mode                      : Normal
Baby Age                        : (not set)
Optical Zoom Mode               : Standard
Conversion Lens                 : Off
```

Travel Day	: n/a
Contrast	: Normal
World Time Location	: Destination
Text Stamp	: Off
Program ISO	: n/a
Advanced Scene Type	: 1
Faces Detected	: 0
Saturation	: Normal
Sharpness	: Normal
Film Mode	: Standard (color)
Color Temp Kelvin	: 0
WB Shift AB	: 0
WB Shift GM	: 0
Flash Curtain	: n/a
Panasonic Image Width	: 3968
Panasonic Image Height	: 2232
AF Point Position	: 0.5 0.5
Num Face Positions	: 0
Maker Note Version	: 0132
Scene Mode	: Off
Flash Fired	: No
Flashpix Version	: 0100
Color Space	: sRGB
Exif Image Width	: 1920
Exif Image Height	: 1080
Interoperability Index	: R98 - DCF basic file (sRGB)
Interoperability Version	: 0100
Sensing Method	: One-chip color area
Scene Type	: Directly photographed
Custom Rendered	: Normal
Exposure Mode	: Auto
Digital Zoom Ratio	: 0
Focal Length In 35mm Format	: 24 mm
Scene Capture Type	: Standard
Gain Control	: High gain up
PrintIM Version	: 0250
Compression	: JPEG (old-style)
Thumbnail Offset	: 12288
Thumbnail Length	: 4454
Encoding Process	: Baseline DCT, Huffman coding
Bits Per Sample	: 8
Color Components	: 3
Y Cb Cr Sub Sampling	: YCbCr4:2:2 (2 1)
Jpg From Raw	: (Binary data 453632 bytes, use -b option to extract)
Make	: Panasonic
Camera Model Name	: DMC-LX3
Strip Offsets	: 4294967295
Orientation	: Horizontal (normal)
Rows Per Strip	: 2250
Strip Byte Counts	: 18270000
Raw Data Offset	: 455168
Distortion Param 02	: 0.010772705078125
Distortion Param 04	: 0.02056884765625
Distortion Scale	: 1
Distortion Correction	: On
Distortion Param 08	: 0.12359619140625
Distortion Param 09	: 0.00579833984375
Distortion Param 11	: -0.02374267578125
Exposure Time	: 1/60
F Number	: 2.0
Exposure Program	: Program AE
Exif Version	: 0221
Date/Time Original	: 2012:08:23 10:22:19
Create Date	: 2012:08:23 10:22:19
Exposure Compensation	: 0
Max Aperture Value	: 2.0
Metering Mode	: Center-weighted average
Flash	: Off, Did not fire
Focal Length	: 5.1 mm
File Source	: Digital Camera
Advanced Scene Mode	: Off
Aperture	: 2.0
Blue Balance	: 2.589354
Image Height	: 2232
Image Width	: 3968
Red Balance	: 1.425856
Scale Factor To 35 mm Equivalent:	4.7
Shutter Speed	: 1/60
Thumbnail Image	: (Binary data 4454 bytes, use -b option to extract)
Circle Of Confusion	: 0.006 mm
Field Of View	: 73.7 deg
Focal Length	: 5.1 mm (35 mm equivalent: 24.0 mm)
Hyperfocal Distance	: 2.04 m
Image Size	: 3968x2232
Light Value	: 5.9
Megapixels	: 8.9

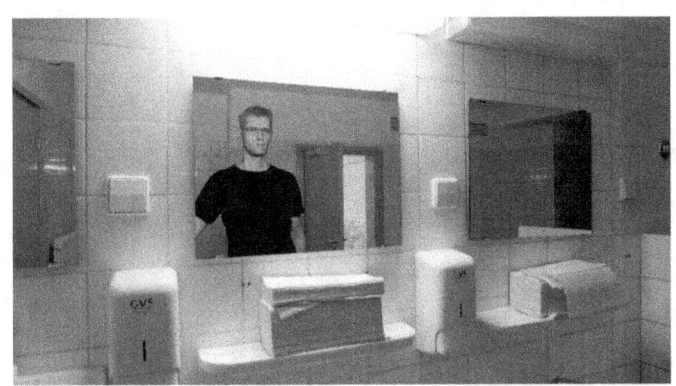

```
ExifTool Version Number         : 10.05
File Name                       : P1050284.RW2
Directory                       : ../Selection
File Size                       : 10 MB
File Modification Date/Time     : 2012:08:23 11:22:44+02:00
File Access Date/Time           : 2015:11:29 14:04:40+01:00
File Inode Change Date/Time     : 2015:11:05 21:35:08+01:00
File Permissions                : rwxrwxrwx
File Type                       : RW2
File Type Extension             : rw2
MIME Type                       : image/x-panasonic-rw2
Exif Byte Order                 : Little-endian (Intel, II)
Panasonic Raw Version           : 0310
Sensor Width                    : 4060
Sensor Height                   : 2250
Sensor Top Border               : 6
Sensor Left Border              : 8
Sensor Bottom Border            : 2238
Sensor Right Border             : 3976
Black Level 1                   : 1
Black Level 2                   : 4
Black Level 3                   : 12
Linearity Limit Red             : 4095
Linearity Limit Green           : 4095
Linearity Limit Blue            : 4095
ISO                             : 250
High ISO Multiplier Red         : 0
High ISO Multiplier Green       : 0
High ISO Multiplier Blue        : 0
Black Level Red                 : 0
Black Level Green               : 0
Black Level Blue                : 0
WB Red Level                    : 392
WB Green Level                  : 263
WB Blue Level                   : 681
Num WB Entries                  : 7
WB Type 1                       : Fine Weather
WB RGB Levels 1                 : 541 256 405
WB Type 2                       : Cloudy
WB RGB Levels 2                 : 601 256 374
WB Type 3                       : Shade
WB RGB Levels 3                 : 666 256 343
WB Type 4                       : Tungsten (Incandescent)
WB RGB Levels 4                 : 361 256 573
WB Type 5                       : Flash
WB RGB Levels 5                 : 613 256 367
WB Type 6                       : D55
WB RGB Levels 6                 : 556 256 410
WB Type 7                       : ISO Studio Tungsten
WB RGB Levels 7                 : 361 256 573
X Resolution                    : 180
Y Resolution                    : 180
Resolution Unit                 : inches
Software                        : Ver.2.2
Modify Date                     : 2012:08:23 10:22:44
Artist                          :
Y Cb Cr Positioning             : Co-sited
Components Configuration        : Y, Cb, Cr, -
Compressed Bits Per Pixel       : 0
Light Source                    : Unknown
Image Quality                   : Raw
Firmware Version                : 0.2.2.0
White Balance                   : Auto
Focus Mode                      : Auto
AF Area Mode                    : 5-area
Image Stabilization             : On, Mode 1
Macro Mode                      : Off
Shooting Mode                   : Program
Audio                           : No
Data Dump                       : (Binary data 8200 bytes, use -b option to extract)
Flash Bias                      : 0
Internal Serial Number          : (F37) 2008:09:24 no. 0023
Panasonic Exif Version          : 0291
Color Effect                    : Off
Time Since Power On             : 00:00:38.21
Burst Mode                      : Off
Sequence Number                 : 0
Contrast Mode                   : Normal
Noise Reduction                 : Standard
Self Timer                      : Off
Rotation                        : Horizontal (normal)
AF Assist Lamp                  : Disabled and Not Required
Color Mode                      : Normal
Baby Age                        : (not set)
Optical Zoom Mode               : Standard
Conversion Lens                 : Off
```

```
Travel Day                          : n/a
Contrast                            : Normal
World Time Location                 : Destination
Text Stamp                          : Off
Program ISO                         : n/a
Advanced Scene Type                 : 1
Faces Detected                      : 0
Saturation                          : Normal
Sharpness                           : Normal
Film Mode                           : Standard (color)
Color Temp Kelvin                   : 0
WB Shift AB                         : 0
WB Shift GM                         : 0
Flash Curtain                       : n/a
Panasonic Image Width               : 3968
Panasonic Image Height              : 2232
AF Point Position                   : 0.5 0.5
Num Face Positions                  : 0
Maker Note Version                  : 0132
Scene Mode                          : Off
Flash Fired                         : No
Flashpix Version                    : 0100
Color Space                         : sRGB
Exif Image Width                    : 1920
Exif Image Height                   : 1080
Interoperability Index              : R98 - DCF basic file (sRGB)
Interoperability Version            : 0100
Sensing Method                      : One-chip color area
Scene Type                          : Directly photographed
Custom Rendered                     : Normal
Exposure Mode                       : Auto
Digital Zoom Ratio                  : 0
Focal Length In 35mm Format         : 24 mm
Scene Capture Type                  : Standard
Gain Control                        : High gain up
PrintIM Version                     : 0250
Compression                         : JPEG (old-style)
Thumbnail Offset                    : 12288
Thumbnail Length                    : 4583
Encoding Process                    : Baseline DCT, Huffman coding
Bits Per Sample                     : 8
Color Components                    : 3
Y Cb Cr Sub Sampling                : YCbCr4:2:2 (2 1)
Jpg From Raw                        : (Binary data 397824 bytes, use -b option to extract)
Make                                : Panasonic
Camera Model Name                   : DMC-LX3
Strip Offsets                       : 4294967295
Orientation                         : Horizontal (normal)
Rows Per Strip                      : 2250
Strip Byte Counts                   : 18270000
Raw Data Offset                     : 399360
Distortion Param 02                 : 0.010772705078125
Distortion Param 04                 : 0.02056884765625
Distortion Scale                    : 1
Distortion Correction               : On
Distortion Param 08                 : 0.12359619140625
Distortion Param 09                 : 0.00579833984375
Distortion Param 11                 : -0.02374267578125
Exposure Time                       : 1/30
F Number                            : 2.0
Exposure Program                    : Program AE
Exif Version                        : 0221
Date/Time Original                  : 2012:08:23 10:22:44
Create Date                         : 2012:08:23 10:22:44
Exposure Compensation               : 0
Max Aperture Value                  : 2.0
Metering Mode                       : Center-weighted average
Flash                               : Off, Did not fire
Focal Length                        : 5.1 mm
File Source                         : Digital Camera
Advanced Scene Mode                 : Off
Aperture                            : 2.0
Blue Balance                        : 2.589354
Image Height                        : 2232
Image Width                         : 3968
Red Balance                         : 1.490494
Scale Factor To 35 mm Equivalent: 4.7
Shutter Speed                       : 1/30
Thumbnail Image                     : (Binary data 4583 bytes, use -b option to extract)
Circle Of Confusion                 : 0.006 mm
Field Of View                       : 73.7 deg
Focal Length                        : 5.1 mm (35 mm equivalent: 24.0 mm)
Hyperfocal Distance                 : 2.04 m
Image Size                          : 3968x2232
Light Value                         : 5.6
Megapixels                          : 8.9
```

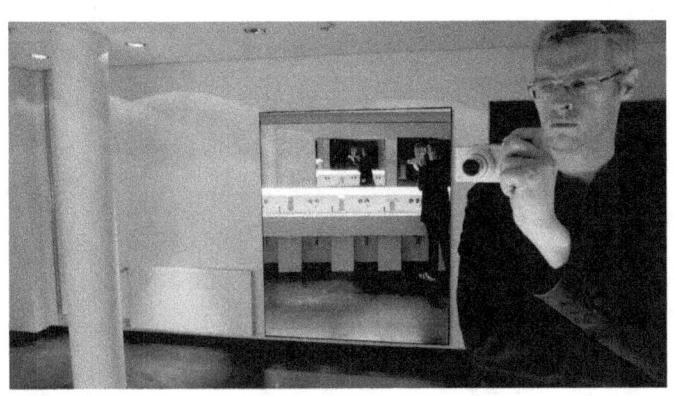

```
ExifTool Version Number         : 10.05
File Name                       : P1060178.RW2
Directory                       : ../Selection
File Size                       : 10 MB
File Modification Date/Time     : 2014:05:11 18:42:26+02:00
File Access Date/Time           : 2015:11:29 14:04:41+01:00
File Inode Change Date/Time     : 2015:11:05 21:35:08+01:00
File Permissions                : rwxrwxrwx
File Type                       : RW2
File Type Extension             : rw2
MIME Type                       : image/x-panasonic-rw2
Exif Byte Order                 : Little-endian (Intel, II)
Panasonic Raw Version           : 0310
Sensor Width                    : 4060
Sensor Height                   : 2250
Sensor Top Border               : 6
Sensor Left Border              : 8
Sensor Bottom Border            : 2238
Sensor Right Border             : 3976
Black Level 1                   : 1
Black Level 2                   : 4
Black Level 3                   : 12
Linearity Limit Red             : 4095
Linearity Limit Green           : 4095
Linearity Limit Blue            : 4095
ISO                             : 320
High ISO Multiplier Red         : 0
High ISO Multiplier Green       : 0
High ISO Multiplier Blue        : 0
Black Level Red                 : 0
Black Level Green               : 0
Black Level Blue                : 0
WB Red Level                    : 380
WB Green Level                  : 263
WB Blue Level                   : 681
Num WB Entries                  : 7
WB Type 1                       : Fine Weather
WB RGB Levels 1                 : 541 256 405
WB Type 2                       : Cloudy
WB RGB Levels 2                 : 601 256 374
WB Type 3                       : Shade
WB RGB Levels 3                 : 666 256 343
WB Type 4                       : Tungsten (Incandescent)
WB RGB Levels 4                 : 361 256 573
WB Type 5                       : Flash
WB RGB Levels 5                 : 613 256 367
WB Type 6                       : D55
WB RGB Levels 6                 : 556 256 410
WB Type 7                       : ISO Studio Tungsten
WB RGB Levels 7                 : 361 256 573
X Resolution                    : 180
Y Resolution                    : 180
Resolution Unit                 : inches
Software                        : Ver.2.2
Modify Date                     : 2014:05:11 16:42:26
Artist                          :
Y Cb Cr Positioning             : Co-sited
Components Configuration        : Y, Cb, Cr, -
Compressed Bits Per Pixel       : 4
Light Source                    : Unknown
Image Quality                   : Raw
Firmware Version                : 0.2.2.0
White Balance                   : Auto
Focus Mode                      : Auto
AF Area Mode                    : 5-area
Image Stabilization             : On, Mode 1
Macro Mode                      : Off
Shooting Mode                   : Program
Audio                           : No
Data Dump                       : (Binary data 8200 bytes, use -b option to extract)
Flash Bias                      : 0
Internal Serial Number          : (F37) 2008:09:24 no. 0023
Panasonic Exif Version          : 0291
Color Effect                    : Off
Time Since Power On             : 00:00:19.19
Burst Mode                      : Off
Sequence Number                 : 0
Contrast Mode                   : Normal
Noise Reduction                 : Standard
Self Timer                      : Off
Rotation                        : Horizontal (normal)
AF Assist Lamp                  : Disabled and Not Required
Color Mode                      : Normal
Baby Age                        : (not set)
Optical Zoom Mode               : Standard
Conversion Lens                 : Off
```

```
Travel Day                          : n/a
Contrast                            : Normal
World Time Location                 : Destination
Text Stamp                          : Off
Program ISO                         : n/a
Advanced Scene Type                 : 1
Faces Detected                      : 0
Saturation                          : Normal
Sharpness                           : Normal
Film Mode                           : Standard (color)
Color Temp Kelvin                   : 0
WB Shift AB                         : 0
WB Shift GM                         : 0
Flash Curtain                       : n/a
Panasonic Image Width               : 3968
Panasonic Image Height              : 2232
AF Point Position                   : 0.5 0.5
Num Face Positions                  : 0
Maker Note Version                  : 0132
Scene Mode                          : Off
Flash Fired                         : No
Flashpix Version                    : 0100
Color Space                         : sRGB
Exif Image Width                    : 1920
Exif Image Height                   : 1080
Interoperability Index              : R98 - DCF basic file (sRGB)
Interoperability Version            : 0100
Sensing Method                      : One-chip color area
Scene Type                          : Directly photographed
Custom Rendered                     : Normal
Exposure Mode                       : Auto
Digital Zoom Ratio                  : 0
Focal Length In 35mm Format         : 24 mm
Scene Capture Type                  : Standard
Gain Control                        : High gain up
PrintIM Version                     : 0250
Compression                         : JPEG (old-style)
Thumbnail Offset                    : 12288
Thumbnail Length                    : 4606
Encoding Process                    : Baseline DCT, Huffman coding
Bits Per Sample                     : 8
Color Components                    : 3
Y Cb Cr Sub Sampling                : YCbCr4:2:2 (2 1)
Jpg From Raw                        : (Binary data 445952 bytes, use -b option to extract)
Make                                : Panasonic
Camera Model Name                   : DMC-LX3
Strip Offsets                       : 4294967295
Orientation                         : Horizontal (normal)
Rows Per Strip                      : 2250
Strip Byte Counts                   : 18270000
Raw Data Offset                     : 447488
Distortion Param 02                 : 0.010772705078125
Distortion Param 04                 : 0.02056884765625
Distortion Scale                    : 1
Distortion Correction               : On
Distortion Param 08                 : 0.12359619140625
Distortion Param 09                 : 0.00579833984375
Distortion Param 11                 : -0.02374267578125
Exposure Time                       : 1/30
F Number                            : 2.0
Exposure Program                    : Program AE
Exif Version                        : 0221
Date/Time Original                  : 2014:05:11 16:42:26
Create Date                         : 2014:05:11 16:42:26
Exposure Compensation               : 0
Max Aperture Value                  : 2.0
Metering Mode                       : Multi-segment
Flash                               : Off, Did not fire
Focal Length                        : 5.1 mm
File Source                         : Digital Camera
Advanced Scene Mode                 : Off
Aperture                            : 2.0
Blue Balance                        : 2.589354
Image Height                        : 2232
Image Width                         : 3968
Red Balance                         : 1.444867
Scale Factor To 35 mm Equivalent    : 4.7
Shutter Speed                       : 1/30
Thumbnail Image                     : (Binary data 4606 bytes, use -b option to extract)
Circle Of Confusion                 : 0.006 mm
Field Of View                       : 73.7 deg
Focal Length                        : 5.1 mm (35 mm equivalent: 24.0 mm)
Hyperfocal Distance                 : 2.04 m
Image Size                          : 3968x2232
Light Value                         : 5.2
Megapixels                          : 8.9
```

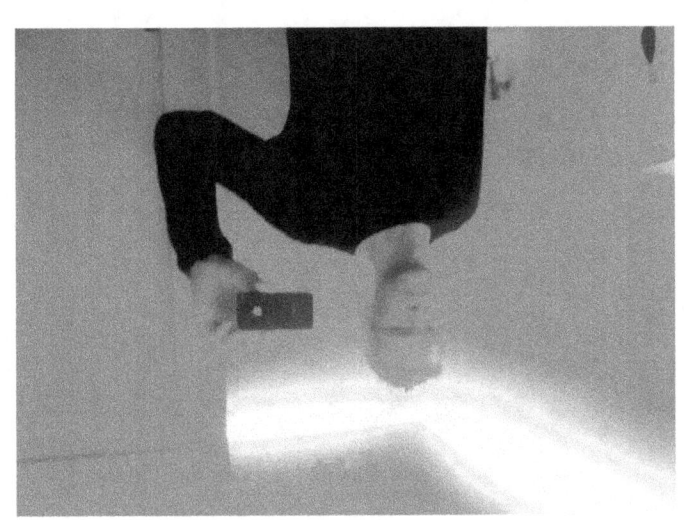

```
ExifTool Version Number         : 10.05
File Name                       : IMG_2346.JPG
Directory                       : ../Selection
File Size                       : 1169 kB
File Modification Date/Time     : 2014:05:14 14:09:41+02:00
File Access Date/Time           : 2015:11:29 14:04:41+01:00
File Inode Change Date/Time     : 2015:11:05 21:35:08+01:00
File Permissions                : rw-------
File Type                       : JPEG
File Type Extension             : jpg
MIME Type                       : image/jpeg
Exif Byte Order                 : Big-endian (Motorola, MM)
Make                            : Apple
Camera Model Name               : iPhone 4
Orientation                     : Rotate 180
X Resolution                    : 72
Y Resolution                    : 72
Resolution Unit                 : inches
Software                        : 7.1.1
Modify Date                     : 2014:05:14 12:09:41
Y Cb Cr Positioning             : Centered
Exposure Time                   : 1/15
F Number                        : 2.8
Exposure Program                : Program AE
ISO                             : 320
Exif Version                    : 0221
Date/Time Original              : 2014:05:14 12:09:41
Create Date                     : 2014:05:14 12:09:41
Components Configuration        : Y, Cb, Cr, -
Shutter Speed Value             : 1/15
Aperture Value                  : 2.8
Brightness Value                : 0.7261640798
Metering Mode                   : Multi-segment
Flash                           : Off, Did not fire
Focal Length                    : 3.9 mm
Subject Area                    : 1295 967 699 696
Run Time Scale                  : 1000000000
Run Time Epoch                  : 0
Run Time Value                  : 678085180781875
Run Time Flags                  : Valid
Sub Sec Time Original           : 371
Sub Sec Time Digitized          : 371
Flashpix Version                : 0100
Color Space                     : sRGB
Exif Image Width                : 2592
Exif Image Height               : 1936
Sensing Method                  : One-chip color area
Scene Type                      : Directly photographed
Exposure Mode                   : Auto
White Balance                   : Auto
Focal Length In 35mm Format     : 35 mm
Scene Capture Type              : Standard
Lens Info                       : 3.85mm f/2.8
Lens Make                       : Apple
Lens Model                      : iPhone 4 back camera 3.85mm f/2.8
GPS Latitude Ref                : North
GPS Longitude Ref               : West
GPS Altitude Ref                : Above Sea Level
GPS Time Stamp                  : 12:09:25.68
Compression                     : JPEG (old-style)
Thumbnail Offset                : 1330
Thumbnail Length                : 5329
Image Width                     : 2592
Image Height                    : 1936
Encoding Process                : Baseline DCT, Huffman coding
Bits Per Sample                 : 8
Color Components                : 3
Y Cb Cr Sub Sampling            : YCbCr4:2:0 (2 2)
Aperture                        : 2.8
GPS Altitude                    : 69.3 m Above Sea Level
GPS Latitude                    : 64 deg 32' 31.56" N
GPS Longitude                   : 21 deg 54' 55.95" W
GPS Position                    : 64 deg 32' 31.56" N, 21 deg 54' 55.95" W
Image Size                      : 2592x1936
Megapixels                      : 5.0
Run Time Since Power Up         : 7 days 20:21:25
Scale Factor To 35 mm Equivalent: 9.1
Shutter Speed                   : 1/15
Create Date                     : 2014:05:14 12:09:41.371
Date/Time Original              : 2014:05:14 12:09:41.371
Thumbnail Image                 : (Binary data 5329 bytes, use -b option to extract)
Circle Of Confusion             : 0.003 mm
Field Of View                   : 54.4 deg
Focal Length                    : 3.9 mm (35 mm equivalent: 35.0 mm)
Hyperfocal Distance             : 1.60 m
Light Value                     : 5.2
```

www.ingramcontent.com/pod-product-compliance
Lightning Source LLC
Chambersburg PA
CBHW082204220526
45470CB00010B/3046